Awaking the Amazing in You

Awakening

the

Amazing

in You

How to
Thrive in
the Midst
of Crisis

New York Times
Best-selling authors

JANET BRAY ATTWOOD
& CHRIS ATTWOOD

WITH 11 TRANSFORMATIONAL LEADERS:
Catherine Allon, Debra Eklove, Rolf Erickson, Ratika Hansen,
Kay McDonald, James Buffalo Moreno, MaryLynn Navarro,
Betsey Sarris, Sue Shalley, Doris Slongo, Debra Stangl

Publishing Consultant: Geoff Affleck, AuthorPreneur Publishing Inc.—geoffaffleck.com
Proofreading: Nina Shoroplova—ninashoroplova.ca
Cover Designer: Pagatana Design Service—pagatana.com
Book Interior and E-book Designer: Amit Dey—amitdey2528@gmail.com

ISBN: 978-0-9755751-3-0 (paperback)
ISBN: 978-0-9755751-4-7 (ebook)

OCC019000 BODY, MIND & SPIRIT / Inspiration & Personal Growth
SEL031000 SELF-HELP / Personal Growth / General

Contents

Introduction

Crisis. It's no fun, but we all seem to run into it from time to time. When those times arrive, it's important to have support, to surround yourself with people who believe in you and will help you get through the tough times.

This book is full of the stories of people like you who've survived crisis and learned from the experience. Their stories will inspire you and their lessons may help guide you through whatever you're going through.

From Janet's finding herself down to thirteen dollars and then making the dramatic decision to give it away to Catherine's perilous escape from Communist Hungary to MaryLynn's incredibly creative process for overcoming the trauma of rape, you'll find yourself enthralled, shocked, delighted, and, at times, in tears, by the stories you'll read here.

Let this book along with the stories and life lessons it contains be your support system. You'll no doubt find yourself on these pages with the map to move through any challenge life may have brought to you.

Permission to Surrender

by Janet Bray Attwood

I remember that fateful day over twenty years ago.
I could feel the tight knot forming in the pit of my stomach.
My head started throbbing, my heart began racing, and my hands instantly became sweaty.

"I can't do it!" I screamed. "God, I need you!" I pleaded. Falling to my knees in front of my computer, I folded my hands, and implored, "Lord, please help me. I can't do this without you!"

I was referring to those horrifying, impossible words, glaring back at me on my computer screen—Merriam-Webster's definition of *surrender*:

transitive verb

1 a: to yield to the power, control, or possession of another upon compulsion or demand

surrendered the fort

b: to give up completely or agree to forgo especially in favor of another

2 a: to give (oneself) up into the power of another especially as a prisoner

b: to give (oneself) over to something (such as an influence)

intransitive verb

: to give oneself up into the power of another: YIELD

To be quite honest, all of Merriam-Webster's definitions of surrender scared the hell out of me, but it was that one insanely unrealistic intransitive verb that really landed like a knife in my belly!

: to give oneself up into the power of another: YIELD

Now, it may seem strange that a dictionary definition could cause such a powerful reaction, but that one word—YIELD—had been the cause of almost all my suffering in life. I knew that I had to surrender to truly be happy, but it seemed impossible.

It was that one damn phrase at the end of all Merriam-Webster's frighteningly painful definitions that jumped out at me in ALL CAPS. It started my pulse racing and my head throbbing the minute I read it.

One thing I have learned is that my body never ever lies to me. Nope, no matter how hard I try to manipulate it, my trusty ol' body will always turn on that terrifying inner GPS alarm the moment one of my biggest fears shows up.

Before reading those definitions and falling to my knees, I had been having one of those absolutely beautiful sunny days. You know the kind I'm talking about. Blue skies, birds overhead, a song-in-your-heart kind of day, when I had the thought, "I should call my friend Julie and have her tell me how I'm doing."

Julie was this super successful intuitive friend of mine. Once she got going and started *clairvoyanting* all over my body, she was always, and I mean ALWAYS right. Within a minute of saying hello, my sweet loving friend Julie ruined it all.

"Janet, what I'm getting is that your greatest lessons in life—and unfortunately, you may not like what I'm going to say because I'm also receiving that the information that's coming will not be easy at all for you—are . . .

"Be patient. Don't push. Let go."

When she said those unwanted, excruciating words to me, the effect was analogous to a PhD trying to teach a newborn the purpose of existence!

Thud.

Letting go and trusting in the Universe were absolutely my all-time greatest fears.

I knew this because I was 100% sure I had never done it. Case in point: four marriages later . . .

My mind was racing. "How could I possibly do that!?" Surrendering for me was like walking in the dark with total blind faith, not knowing where the next safe footing would be, afraid that the unknown would unveil more than I could ever take.

"No," I thought. "It's far worse than that. It's actually death. Yup, death for sure."

"So, Janet," Julie continued. "I want to give you some instructions so that this isn't so hard. What I want you to do is get out a piece of paper and pen after I leave, go back in your past, and try to locate a time when you had to let go."

"Uh, okay," I stammered, not really believing that a moment in time like that had ever existed for me.

"Why do you think I want you to do that?" Julie continued.

"So I'll know it's possible?" I stammered.

"Yup," Julie smiled. "Okay. I'll check in with you tomorrow. Happy writing."

"Uh-huh," I said, as I sat at my desk, with absolutely no thoughts in my brain; none whatsoever. Lacking any idea what to write, I had gone to Merriam-Webster's dictionary. Ugh. Absolutely no help.

···◆◆◆···

It's a funny thing about setting an intention and getting down on one's knees. Sometimes, the Universe is actually listening.

As I sat there at my desk, I pushed my computer aside, picked up my pen, took a deep breath, closed my eyes, and then, miraculously, it happened. A memory started flooding in. I could hardly write fast enough.

One of my first experiences of consciously giving myself permission to hand it all over to the Universe was in 1980. I had a job recruiting disk drive engineers in Silicon Valley and was failing miserably. The worst part of all was that everyone who worked there was my friend. Luckily for me, one day after work when I was meditating in the local meditation center, I opened my eyes and glanced up at a sign on the bulletin board that advertised a success seminar called "Yes to Success." It was to be held in San Francisco the following weekend.

All circuits firing, I knew that somehow the answer to my prayers had everything to do with taking that seminar. My intuition couldn't have been more on! Not only did I take the seminar, but I eventually persuaded the seminar leader, a vivacious and passionate woman named Debra Poneman, to hire me. As luck would have it, Debra was going on her US speaking tour at the same time I was to arrive in Los Angeles where her company was located, and she needed someone to house-sit. She said I could stay in her apartment, study her success tapes while she was gone and, when she returned, I could start my illustrious career, uplifting and speaking to hundreds of people all over the world. I was in seventh heaven!

Two weeks later, after Debra and I finalized our plans, I said goodbye to all my friends at the recruiting firm in Silicon Valley, packed my bags, filled my vintage red Toyota up with gas, and headed down to Los Angeles, radio blaring, singing at the top of my lungs, ecstatic that I was on my way to start my dream career.

Two miles into my journey, my little red Toyota started sputtering and spurting. Steam started pouring out of the hood of my precious car and as I was pulling over to the side of the freeway to see what was going on, my trusty little red car took one big, shuddering breath and let out the most God-awful sound. Right there, on the US Route 101, my little trusty red Toyota died.

Horrified, I sat frozen by the side of the freeway, stunned at what had just happened.

Once the initial shock of losing my beloved Toyota wore off, I came up with an alternate plan to take a train to Los Angeles. After paying the tow truck to tow my car, buying my train ticket to Los Angeles, and then taking a long taxi ride to Debra's apartment in Santa Monica, to my dismay and alarm, I arrived at Debra's door with $13.00 left to my name.

Frozen with fear that Debra wouldn't hire me to go out and teach other people her success principles if she knew I was completely broke, I said nothing while we were together and kept a sunny smile on my face until Debra finally waved her last goodbye to me.

Now what am I going to do? I thought to myself. I felt totally weighed down by the fact that I had hardly enough money to last me more than a few days. Depressed, I did what any future success trainer would do in a situation like this: I went to Debra's refrigerator and scooped myself a huge double serving of her chocolate ice cream. After eating almost the entire half gallon, I lay down on her couch and fell into a drunken, chocolate-induced sleep.

When I awoke, I decided there was only one option when things got this bad. Meditation.

I grabbed the keys to Debra's blue Chevy (that she had told me I could borrow for emergencies only) and headed down the Coast Highway wondering what the heck I was going to do next.

Arriving at a gorgeous meditation center in Malibu, I immediately felt a deep sense of calm envelop me. I walked past all the beautiful buildings to the majestic and serene gardens that graced this special place. I sat down on one of the wooden benches by the path to contemplate my sorry state.

As I sat there, I noticed a little wooden donation box attached to a post near the bench. *What is $13.00 really going to do for me anyway?* I asked myself. *Pretty much nothing,* I realized. So, reaching into my purse, I pulled out my treasured, crisp one-dollar bills and stuffed the last $13.00 I had left to my name into that little wooden box.

Having donated every penny I had, I sat down again on the bench and had a very intimate talk with God. I poured out my heart and told Him all that was going on with me, pointing out where I could use some of Her/His support.

After a little while, I walked back to Debra's car, knowing that letting go of all the money I had left in the world absolutely had to be the best thing I could have ever done. I didn't know why I felt that way, but I did.

Halfway to Debra's house, the huge realization of what I had just done hit me right in the gut. *You stupid idiot!* I thought to myself. *Are you kidding me?! You absolute mood-maker. Did you really just give your last $13.00 away to a wooden box? What were you thinking?!!*

Immediately, I felt despair and fear. *What the heck am I going to do now?!!*

I headed back to Debra's apartment and the minute I walked in, the phone rang.

"Hello," I said.

"Janet, is that you?"

"Uh-huh. Who's this?" I asked.

"It's me, Francis."

Francis is my ex-husband, Terry's father, whom I totally love and I hadn't heard from in over a year.

"Hi, Francis, it's so nice to hear from you. How did you know where to get a hold of me?" I asked.

"Terry said Andrew was talking to your sister Mickey and she said you were starting a new career as a speaker and had just arrived in Santa Monica. She gave me your number."

After we chatted on the phone for some time, Francis invited me to meet him for lunch at a nearby restaurant. *Well, at least I'll get to eat one more meal*, I thought to myself.

"Sure, Francis," I told him. "I'd love to."

As we were sitting at the restaurant, Francis was becoming more and more passionate and animated, talking a hundred miles a minute. He shared that he had just started selling a natural weight-loss program he was really excited about. With that, he took out the big paper bag he had brought in with him and plopped four bottles of the stuff he was telling me about on the table. Simultaneously, with a huge grin on his face, he proclaimed to me, "Janet, this is just the beginning for you. From now on, as God is my witness, money is going to absolutely flow to you, just like it has for me."

Hardly taking a breath, Francis kept on. "Janet," he said, "I think this is something you could really make a lot of money on in your spare time, if you wanted to."

I adored Francis. Even though it had been a year since I'd seen him, he still had that same beautiful sparkle in his eyes and infectious way about him. Today was no exception, and when he spoke about the products he had set down before me, I couldn't help but start to feel excited about them too.

"The opportunity sounds great," I said. "How about when I have some extra money, I'll order some from you?"

"I don't think you should wait that long," Francis said to me, still smiling from ear to ear.

"It just so happens that I have five hundred dollars' worth of this great stuff in the trunk of my car. You can have these bottles on the table and the five hundred dollars' worth as well. Pay me back after you sell them and make some money for yourself. Wouldn't that be great, Janet?"

"Oh, Francis, you have no idea."

And with that, Francis set the four bottles right in front of me. Not more than two seconds passed when our very overweight server walked up to our table, eyed the bottles, and said to me, "What's that?"

"What's that?!" I exclaimed. "This is one of the best organic weight-loss programs you will ever, ever find. And not only that,"

I continued, "You can create an income for yourself while you eat your way to your ideal weight by sharing it with others. How good is that?"

I quickly glanced in Francis's direction to see if I was saying it all in the way he had shared. Francis quickly gave me a big thumbs up and I continued on, telling our server absolutely everything I could possibly remember that he had just told me. When I was finally done, she blurted out, "I'll take everything you have!" and immediately she whipped out a hundred dollar bill from her apron, grabbed the bottles, and walked away.

I sat there absolutely stunned and overjoyed at what had just happened.

Thanking Francis as we said goodbye, I headed home.

···✦◆✦···

As I was writing about this experience of letting go and surrendering, I realized that that particular experience had actually been a profound lesson for me. One which, many years later, I am still learning from.

"Oh my God," I thought. "I can do it. I did do it, and now I just have to keep doing it."

For one precious moment, I realized that I have always been taken care of. Giving myself permission to trust and donating my last thirteen dollars was my way of surrendering to that unseen force that is always looking after each of us. By accessing that memory from ages ago, I learned that all that's required of me is to let go of my own agenda and surrender to God / Nature / Higher Power's plan, melting into that energy that is greater than myself. I saw that when I do that, the result is always better than what I can come up with on my own.

As tears streamed down my face, I promised myself, that from this day forward I would never look back, but instead, I would trust that each time I arrived at a new fork in the road, no matter what happened, I would simply remind myself that if it worked for me then, it will work for me now.

Fast forward twenty years.

I've gone on to speak to millions of people around the world, and I eventually wrote my book, *The Passion Test*, with my partner, Chris Attwood. To my amazement and delight, it went on to become a *New York Times* best seller. So many other amazing experiences have happened that there are too many to share. Thanks to my growing ability to surrender, my life has become better than anything I could ever have imagined.

intransitive verb

: to give oneself up into the power of another: YIELD

···◆◆◆···

Ha! You aren't that scary after all.

IMPORTANT NOTE TO READER: This story is not an invitation to give away your last few dollars and hope something good will happen. Please don't do that unless you feel with all your heart that it is the right thing to do and you're willing to take 100% responsibility for whatever happens next. Don't come back and say, "But she told me if I give away all my money something good will happen." I didn't and that is NOT surrender. That is blame and that will not get you to a joy-filled life.

This story IS an invitation to get curious about your answers to the following questions:

- *Where are you hanging on to your concepts of what has to happen in your life?*

- *Where are you trying to control what happens to you?*

- *Where are you resisting the force of evolution that is asking you to let go?*

- *How can you allow the infinite organizing power of Nature (or, if you prefer, the divine) to take over your life?*

Janet Bray Attwood *is the New York Times best-selling author of* The Passion Test *and* Your Hidden Riches. *As an expert and featured speaker on what it takes to live a passionate life, she has presented her programs to hundreds of thousands of people around the world, sharing the stage with people like the 14th Dalai Lama, Sir Richard Branson, Nobel Laureate F. W. de Klerk, Stephen Covey, former Zappos CEO Tony Hsieh, T. Harv Eker, Jack Canfield, Brendon Burchard, and others.*

Janet has taken hundreds of thousands of people through The Passion Test process all over the world. She is the co-founder of the Passion Test Certification Program, which has over 4500+ Certified Facilitators in more than 65 countries. Janet is also the co-founder of other programs: The Passion Test for Business, The Passion Test for Kids & Teens, Enlightened Bestseller, The Passion Test Reclaim Your Power Program for the homeless, and The Mastery of Self Love.

Janet co-founded one of the first online magazines, Healthy Wealthy nWise. *Prior to becoming a top transformational leader, Janet worked in the corporate world. In one of her positions, she was the marketing director for the third largest book buyer in the United States, "Books Are Fun," managing the marketing department of over forty marketers. It was during her tenure there that the company was purchased by* Reader's Digest *for $360 million.*

Janet is a facilitator of "The Work of Byron Katie." She is also a facilitator of the environmental symposium, "Awakening the Dreamer: Changing the Dream" and a "Certified Strategic Synchronicity Leader." You can contact Janet at **support@ thepassiontest.com** *and learn more about her programs at* **thepassiontest.com.**

Discovering and Releasing Your Core Wounds

The first and most basic step toward
fulfillment and happiness

by Debra Stangl

"I'm here!" I felt a wave of relief wash over me as I entered the spiritual mecca of Sedona, Arizona, for the first time. That was over twenty years ago.

My life was a mess—I had just started my twentieth year as a divorce attorney, a profession I hated. I was in an unhappy marriage, forty pounds overweight, and $50,000 in debt from bad business decisions my now ex-husband had made but for which I was jointly responsible. I was burned out, stressed out, frustrated, and unhappy, and I felt completely stuck. I saw no way out . . . until I came to Sedona.

Little did I know that two weeks later, $50,000 would fall out of the sky. Six months after that I would leave my law practice, and in 2002 I would start Sedona Soul Adventures, doing the work of my dreams. Along the way, I would release over forty pounds in five weeks without diet or exercise, manifest a loving relationship and marry the man of my dreams, plus write an international #1 best-selling book entitled *The Journey to Happy: How Embracing the Concept That "Nothing Is Wrong" Can Transform Your Life.*

What? How did all that happen? How did this relatively normal, middle-aged woman go from frustrated and deeply unhappy to blissed out and living the life of her dreams? The short answer is that I finally found and released my Core Wounds.

Even though I had been on my spiritual path since my mother's untimely death in 1978, I didn't realize that even with all the spiritual work I had done, I had never really dealt with my Core Wounds. I didn't even know exactly what that meant, other than having a very basic understanding of those words.

So I'm going to share with you what Core Wounds are, how they're affecting you and showing up in your life, and give you some thoughts and ideas on how to discover and release your own.

What Is a Core Wound?

In my work over the past twenty years, I've dealt with all types of people—celebrities, politicians, regular folks, rich and poor, straight and gay—and what I've found is that at the core of each person I've ever met is a wound that is doing everything it can on an energetic level to get itself healed. It's bringing in painful experiences, difficult people, and sometimes even illness to get us to finally look it in the face, recognize it, embrace it, and heal it.

Until I dealt with my Core Wounds, they were showing up consistently in every area of my life:

- No matter what I did to lose weight (strict diets, manic exercise), my body was never exactly the way I wanted it.

- No matter how hard I worked, I wasn't reaching the kind of success that I had dreamed of.

- No matter how I approached relationships (including being married to husbands who were supportive both emotionally and financially), I never received the kind of love I truly wanted and never felt satisfied.

- Even though I was an attorney and brought in substantial income, I never had the financial resources that I wanted. Money seemed to slip through my fingers, and there was never enough.

That's the insidious thing about Core Wounds—until they're healed, they keep showing up in all areas of your life. That's because they're screaming, begging to be healed.

In your life, do you have the feeling that you're not good enough? Not smart enough? That no matter what you do, it's never enough? When you see the word *enough* keep coming up in your thoughts, that's a good sign your Core Wounds are lurking just underneath them.

How Does the Wounding Happen?

For most people, the Wounds stem from events in childhood, and very often people remember them because they're so jarring. There are also those (like me) who believe that some Core Wounds are brought into our current lifetime from a past life.

It's All a Cosmic Setup

Through lots of personal work, I discovered the two events that created my Core Wounds. The first was a past life in ancient Egypt, and the second was in this lifetime, but both were completely connected.

In 1989 I was in a ninety-day outpatient Twelve Step Program for Adult Children of Alcoholics. We did a process where we were told, "By doing this process you are going to discover the event that caused you to be here in this program, caused your unhappiness, sent you to therapy, and so on. We'll go through each year of your life starting at the age of sixteen. Think quickly about what happened to you when you were that age, and then we'll go to the previous year. We'll go in descending order, and for most of you, the key event happened between the ages of four and seven."

We did the process and I mined each year, thinking that it would be connected to my father's alcoholism, which really started kicking in when I was around eleven. I'd always believed it had caused most of the trouble in my life (remember, this was being done as part of a Twelve Step Program for Adult Children of Alcoholics). But as I dredged up memories of those years, I could see them, but nothing was happening—no emotion, no reaction.

Suddenly, we got to age five and memories started flooding back. I was in kindergarten. I had started dance lessons at age three and I was about to debut in my first solo performance at the kindergarten Christmas pageant. My mother was nine months pregnant with my sister, and in my five-year-old naivete, I was begging my mother to just "make it through" so she could be there at my performance. Of course, on the big day I awoke to the house in turmoil and my mother on the phone to the hospital telling them she was on her way, while my dad was getting the car warmed up.

As I saw these images, I started sobbing and sobbing, my body wracking itself with the pain of these memories. *This can't be it,* I thought. *This makes no sense, this can't be what created all this pain for me.*

But it was. I felt so completely abandoned, so lost, so not loved or cared about. Despite all the therapy and energy healing I'd done prior to that moment, I had no idea of the damage that was unintentionally inflicted on my psyche that day. Of course my mother never intended to hurt me—she was in labor! But as a five-year-old, I didn't have the ability to understand that. Instead, I unconsciously absorbed those feelings of not being loved, and the wounds went in. *I'm not good enough for her to come to the pageant. She doesn't love me enough to come to the pageant. I can never have what I want. I'll never be happy.* Do any of these feelings sound familiar to you?

When I discovered this, I had no idea that I would later unearth an even deeper meaning and cause. Fast forward six years later. I was about to go to Egypt for the second time. I rarely get sick, yet one day, when I suddenly and inexplicably became very ill, I knew that something was up. My husband at the time was a master at applied kinesiology, especially using closed-ended questions to get yes and no answers. He spent hours asking me these questions, and because we were so close to going on the Egypt trip, he asked,

- Is this connected to the Egypt trip? *Yes.*
- A particular day? *Yes.*

We went through the entire itinerary and the muscle testing said yes to the day in Karnak.

- Did I live in Karnak in a past life? *Yes*

You can imagine how long and how many questions it took to bring out the entire story. And amazingly, over the years, I can't tell you how many psychics and intuitives have told me the same story—without my having told them anything about it. I've also visited this story in hypnosis and seen visions of it in many, many breathwork journeys.

Here's the story: I wasn't anyone famous, just a young priestess in a cult in Karnak who fell in love with a priest, which was forbidden. He was teaching us to use energy to control other people, showing us ways to avoid our heart chakra so that we would have no empathy or caring for the people we were trying to control. It all ended very badly—I became pregnant, he was executed, and I saved myself by allowing the cult to use my baby daughter (my sister in this lifetime) in a ritual sacrifice.

It's important to note that the ancient Egyptians did not practice human sacrifice, but this secret cult did.

On the day in this current lifetime when my sister was born, her soul somehow ingeniously dealt with this karma in one fell swoop. I had allowed them to kill her in the previous lifetime. When she came into this lifetime, she did so in a way that totally messed me up—by giving me wounds of "I'm not good enough," "there's something wrong with me," and "I can't ever be happy"—issues that I dealt with for years and years. And her soul did it in an amazingly elegant way—not by killing me or doing anything else that would keep the karma going, but just through the perfect timing of her birth.

What Happens When the Wounds Go In?

When these events happen, we really "get it" that we are separate from unconditional love. Our connection to Source has been disturbed, so it's a jolt. Suddenly something is wrong.

Of course we don't have the cognition when we're young to say to ourselves, "I've just disconnected from Source and unconditional love." Instead, it becomes "something is wrong with *me*."

And I believe that feeling starts a search on a soul level to heal the disconnection and wounding so that we can come back into knowing that All Is Well and Nothing Is Wrong, and return to being in constant connection with Source and All That Is.

Some people embark on that search for healing and some people don't. Some people go through their entire lives in disconnection and unhappiness and emptiness.

For me, the wounds went in deep, and they kept showing up throughout my life in all their "not enoughness" with me feeling that "I'll never be happy." They manifested in my discontent with my work, my unhappiness in my marriages, my struggles with my body, and my financial troubles.

How Can You Discover Your Core Wounds?

The good news is that the key to the healing is in the Core Wound itself! That's the beauty of it—that's where the discovery is. You don't have to look any further than at the painful parts of your life.

Look at the basic areas of your life—your body, health, work, money, relationships, and overall enjoyment of life. When you look at these different areas, how are they? Are you what the world would call *successful*? Have you *succeeded* in all of these areas? Have you done well and are you happy and satisfied with where you are in all of these areas? Are you content?

If the answer is no, where do you feel dissatisfied? Can you find patterns that you keep repeating?

If your relationships are unsatisfying, do you seem to attract the same kind of people over and over again? In my situation, I kept attracting men who were unavailable emotionally and who couldn't support themselves financially.

How about your money situation? Does money slip through your fingers? Are you able to save? Do you feel secure financially? Do you love your body? Do you take care of it? Do you trust it? Is it your friend? Or are you at odds? Do you love your work? Or is it a grind? Are you living your life's purpose? Are you successful? Or do you find that you trip yourself up?

Look at these areas and identify the ones that bother you the most or that show up as patterns. And then look at how you talk about these things. How do you think about these things? Are you engaging in negative self-talk?

Do you say things to yourself like these?

- I am so stupid (or *You are so stupid*),
- No matter what I do . . . (fill in the blank).
- There's never enough . . . (fill in the blank: money, time, etc.).
- I'll never be able to . . . (fill in the blank).

At the root of all this is what I call the *enoughness* factor. It's all about *not enough: I'm not good enough, I'm not smart enough, there's not enough time, not enough money, not enough love.* Are any of those showing up for you?

And then there are the wounds that are more basic—*I'm not loveable, there's something wrong with me, no one understands me.*

Keep digging, and you'll get to the root—you'll get down to the basic wound. And chances are, it's showing up in every part of your life.

How Do I Heal My Core Wounds?

Once you've found them, what do you do with them? Although it really helps to know what the Core Wounds are, I've never found that just knowing about them was enough to have their destructive nature quelled.

Core Wounds go into us in such a deep way that they become part of our energy, part of our cellular makeup. They affect us on all levels—physical, mental, emotional, spiritual—so just *knowing* what they are, just having that knowledge satisfied on the mental level, doesn't do much to help the other levels. They're literally still in your body, still affecting your emotions and your beliefs (the spiritual aspect).

For me, the healing of my Core Wounds took a long time. I think part of this was because I wasn't focused on healing my Core Wounds. I just knew that I was unhappy and didn't feel good, and I wanted to change things. Initially, when I came to Sedona in 1999, the first thing that happened was I had a vision in which I was told I had to leave my law practice and change my life. Given that I was $50,000 in debt, had no money in savings, and was the sole supporter of my family, I didn't see with my conscious brain how that was possibly going to happen. So I spent the next two weeks with my lawyer brain trying to figure it out. Which, of course, didn't work.

Suddenly, at the end of those two weeks, during a meditation, I made a promise to myself and to God that I was going to do this. I didn't know how that was going to happen, I just knew I had to do it. As I made the promise to God, I said, "But I need some help." At that moment, I felt this wave of surrender come over me. Rather than feeling anxious and worried about how I was going to figure things out, I felt serene.

A few hours later, one of my former clients called me. His case was finished, so I don't even remember why he was calling. At the end of our conversation he told me he had just bought a new business refinancing mortgages. I asked him if I could get my mortgage payment reduced. He called back in ten minutes, saying, "I can get your mortgage payment cut in half. And I can get you $50,000 in cash."

Suddenly, the weight of this debt I'd been holding for five years was gone. Six months later, I closed my law office completely and spent an entire month in Sedona, doing work with different practitioners. Over the next three years, I was coming to Sedona approximately half the time, staying for a month at a time to do sessions with different practitioners. Although I wasn't calling it Core Wound work, looking back now, I see that's what it turned out to be. We just kept digging and releasing, digging and releasing, digging and releasing.

Two years in, I had an epiphany. Up until that time, I used to have this negative self-talk of "If I die tomorrow, I'd be so angry because I would feel like there has never been a point in my life when I felt truly happy." One day I was in my kitchen in Omaha looking out the window and watching the beautiful tall trees swaying in the wind. I felt the same kind of serenity as I had the day the $50,000 fell out of the sky, and I suddenly had the thought, "If I die tomorrow, it would be okay."

Two weeks before 9/11, I was in Sedona again doing a session and my Higher Self appeared to me for the second time in a vision, as she had done almost two years before in the exact same place. She said, "It's time to move to Sedona."

"To do what?" I replied.

No response.

My experience is that we're never shown the whole picture, only the next step. By this time, I knew I had to do as I was told. I sold my house in three days (the realtor said it would take six months) for $30,000 more than the listing price.

I moved to Sedona and sat there for six months, saying to the Universe, "I did what you told me to do, now what?" Then I started having the same dream. I was shown that working with these amazing practitioners one-on-one is what had transformed my life and that I could create an experience which could do that for other people. I was shown it could happen in three days, and that proved to be true. In fact, twenty years later, the joke at my office is that my Sedona Soul Adventure took three years, but everyone else does it in three days. The difference, of course, is that now we're laser focused on discovering and clearing the Core Wounds and then bringing each person back into connection on all the levels—physical, mental, emotional, and spiritual. Discovering and clearing the Core Wounds is key and, with our retreats, we can uncover them in a single session and heal them in a single retreat. But it's been a fascinating process and it's taught me so much about helping others.

Along the way, other miracles happened. I had struggled with my weight my entire life, and when I first came to Sedona, I was more than forty pounds overweight. On the day this particular miracle happened, my now ex-husband and I got into an argument. The argument devolved into what it always did—namely, that it was never okay for me to get angry with him. No matter what he did or didn't do, it was his position that it was never okay for me to get angry.

After this argument, I went home and started crying. I got into bed and suddenly I started vibrating—to the point where I couldn't move. I heard a voice in my head saying over and over again, "Nothing is wrong with you, nothing is wrong with you, nothing is wrong with you." All at once I was shown how in every area of my life, nothing was wrong. That it was just my perception—how I was looking at it and my resistance to it—that was causing the problem.

Very specifically, I was shown that nothing was wrong with my body. Once the vibrations ceased, I jumped out of bed feeling elated and made the decision to stop the crazy diet I was on (no carbs plus manic exercise) and feed my body what it wanted, no matter what it was. Five weeks later, I went shopping for blue jeans and suddenly discovered I had gone from a size 14 to a size 6. I went home and weighed myself and found I had released over forty pounds simply by loving my body, no longer thinking there was anything wrong with it, by eating and drinking whatever I wanted, whenever I wanted it.

Not only had the Core Wounds been released, but I had moved completely into the deep knowing that nothing was wrong with me. That understanding was reflected directly in my body. My husband, however, did not agree with that assessment and we divorced about a year after that. He had fed my belief that something was wrong with me, and when I realized that it wasn't true, our energies simply didn't mesh any longer.

The final miracle happened a few years later when I utilized all I had learned and taught in order to bring in the man of my dreams. You know that the Core Wounds have been healed when your life reflects it—by loving your body, loving your partner, loving your work, living in abundance, and finally feeling full and satisfied.

After working with people for over forty years (first as a family law attorney and now with Sedona Soul Adventures), I am convinced that all of us have Core Wounds, and until we discover and clear them, we're incapable of truly experiencing the joy and bliss that I believe is our birthright.

The Process

It doesn't need to take years. Try this:

- Sit with yourself and start breathing deeply.
- Look at the different areas in your life. Core Wounds show up in our problems, our struggles, our dissatisfactions, in the things we don't have in our lives that we want.
- Look specifically at your body, health, work, money, relationships, and overall enjoyment of life. Where are you? Where are the struggles? Journal about this in each area, focusing on where you are and where you want to be.
- After journaling, do some more deep breaths and allow memories to surface about times when things "went wrong" or when an incident made you feel "less than." Take a deep breath and ask for a memory. See what bubbles up first and record this in your journal.

What are your feelings accompanying the memory? What are the thoughts? Some examples might be these:

- I'm not good enough.
- I'm not enough.
- Something is wrong with me.
- Nobody cares.
- I hate myself.

- I don't matter.
- I'm unlovable.
- I'm afraid of being rejected (or abandoned or vulnerable, etc.).

When a thought comes up, you've nailed it—you know what your Core Wound is.

Look for the patterns in your life to see how this is showing up. For example, if your Core Wound is "I'm unlovable," your love relationships probably are not working out.

Now that you know what your Core Wound is, the next step is clearing it. Sometimes we can do that on our own, but sometimes we need help, especially if the energy is really stuck.

The healing comes about through clearing the pain and the wound, and moving into self-love and acceptance. Effective methods to use on your own are such things as Tapping, EMDR (Eye Movement Desensitization and Reprocessing), guided meditation, and affirmations. It's all about moving into the energy of unconditionally loving and accepting every part of yourself.

The clearing part will take some time and effort. You'll start to see the effects as you look at your life. Are some of the patterns moving? Have you stopped the negative self-talk? Are you unconditionally loving yourself?

This is the key—invite in unconditional love.

Enjoy your new life of unconditional loving!!

Debra Stangl is an example of how life is full of second chances. After practicing law for over twenty years in Omaha, Nebraska, Debra had a spiritual reawakening in Sedona in 1999. Moving to Sedona in 2001 and founding Sedona Soul Adventures in 2002, Debra developed the unique process of deeply transformational, private retreats that are custom-designed for individuals and couples (not groups), utilizing over fifty of Sedona's Master Practitioners.

Sedona Soul Adventures was named "Best of Sedona" for Retreats in 2020, 2021, and 2022; named Best Marriage Retreat in the US from 2017 to 2022; featured in The Washington Post, USA Today, the Today show, Forbes, *and* Yoga Journal; *and became one of the Inc. 5000 List of Fastest-Growing Private Companies in the US in 2019.*

Debra leads group trips each year to Egypt and Machu Picchu, and she is the author of the #1 International Best Seller The Journey to Happy: How Embracing the Concept That "Nothing Is Wrong" Can Transform Your Life. *You may reach Debra at Debra@SedonaSoulAdventures.com*

Reinventing Remarkable

by Ratika Hansen

"Good morning. And what is your name?" I asked the first boy I saw standing outside my office door. He looked excited, eager, and curious about what was about to happen. He also appeared, as I expected, somewhat confused by my simple question.

"Samir," he answered in a quizzical tone, his head cocked to one side.

I checked my Day One roster with an air of officiality and gave him a confirming nod.

Then I leaned over to speak to the second boy. "So then you must be . . . Sanjay? Am I saying that right?" as I purposely over-enunciated his name.

"Yes," he replied with an amused look and more confidence than the first boy.

"Welcome to Hansen Summer Camp! Come on in," I said, opening the door and smiling at each of them as they giggled about our inside joke.

As my twin boys entered my home office to kick off our homegrown camp, I rejoiced in the laughter, fun, and surprise

I had in store for them while the rest of the world endured a pandemic lockdown.

Creating Hansen Summer Camp was my first experience of what I now call Reinventing Remarkable, an approach to overcome the challenges I encountered during the COVID-19 pandemic. The results have been beyond what I ever dreamed they could be. I'm sharing these success stories of my Reinventing Remarkable with the hope that you will be inspired to create versions of Remarkable in your life, too.

Hansen Summer Camp: Now Open!

In the few weeks prior to the Hansen Summer Camp kickoff, it had become painfully apparent that I wouldn't be able to rely on our usual summer camp for childcare this year. Like so many other local businesses, it had closed its doors, leaving me to wonder how I would manage to take care of my boys, do my job well from home, and maintain some semblance of sanity.

Homeschooling was hard enough when the pandemic first hit, even though my children's teacher taught them online for part of the day. With summer break on the horizon, how was I going to keep them entertained, out of each other's hair—and, frankly, out of mine—all day, every day, with no other support at home? I resigned to accept reality and decided to continue a version of the homeschooling schedule that we had finally landed on after weeks of tweaking. In my eyes, summer vacation was going to be an extension of the school year, and I was okay with that.

"But this is our summer vacation, Mommy!" my boys protested when I casually presented my plan. "It can't be just like the school year!" Their honesty made it clear that the last three months had taken a toll on their playful little spirits and they were hungry for respite. As it was, they were being denied the summer camp experience that they looked forward to every year. And on top of that, was I going to make it a diluted version of school? What was I thinking? And so Hansen Summer Camp was born. I promptly got to work.

I sat down with my "campers" and we brainstormed weekly themes, discussed camp rules, and created a schedule of daily activities. They were so excited, sometimes talking over each other and going entirely too fast for me to keep up. I may have gone a bit overboard, buying lanyards, making weekly theme-based name tags, and designing personalized camp guidebooks. But if they weren't going to their regular camp, then they were going to get full-on camp at home!

Each morning, I kissed them "goodbye" and then they assembled outside my office, eagerly awaiting "Mrs. Hansen's" arrival. I greeted them with the cheery face that seems to be part of a camp counselor's job description and asked them how they were—as if I had not just seen them. We kicked off each day with a camp song from my own Girl Scouts camp songbook from eons ago, rocking back and forth, and clapping our hands. The sillier the songs, the harder they tried to follow along and memorize the words. It was a trip back to my childhood every morning and arguably set me up for a more joyful day, too. Then we meditated and did a little bit of schoolwork in our attempt to conquer the academic summer slide. After that, while the schedule was similar each day, the activities were based on the week's theme.

At the end of each day, if they had followed the schedule, they earned a sticker reflecting the week's theme. Oh, how they looked forward to those stickers! I learned quickly that stickers go a long way when you are eight years old. Every Friday, they wrote about their favorite memories from the week in their camp guidebook and listed the books they had read that week as well. At the end of the summer, I presented them with Certificates of Completion and they rewarded me with big hugs, as if to say, "Well done, Mrs. Hansen!" My heart swelled with admiration for my boys as I looked back at how they displayed mature resilience and boundless creativity in the face of huge disappointment.

The proof was in the pudding as we headed into Summer 2021. They requested, or rather *expected*, an encore of Hansen Summer Camp. As we brainstormed new themes and activities, they were more excited than ever! Never had I imagined designing a summer camp curriculum for my boys, but my efforts showed me what magic is possible when we refuse to settle and instead open ourselves to the prospect of going beyond "okay"—when we strive for Remarkable.

My Friend Phyllis

We began the new school year after our first Hansen Summer Camp, and six months later the Universe delivered another opportunity for me to Reinvent Remarkable.

"That feels like a fibroid," my doctor said, quite assuredly. "A big one."

Hmm, I thought. *Fibroids are made of uterine tissue. But I don't have a uterus. So how could that be a fibroid? And if it isn't a fibroid, then what is it?*

Fortunately, when it comes to my health, I'm predisposed to wait for confirmed bad news before panicking. So I bided my time in a (mostly) calm and positive space while also preparing myself for whatever news might come. To my relief, two weeks later an ultrasound confirmed that it was indeed just a fibroid. I was relieved to have a somewhat common diagnosis and a referral to a very reputable surgeon in the field. But as common as the diagnosis was, I knew I was not a typical case, so I was open to any extra expertise I could get.

In the months leading up to my surgery, my pelvic therapist-cum-energy worker encouraged me to meditate and talk to my fibroid, preparing it to leave my body wholly and completely. It was getting larger and more uncomfortable by the day, so I was eager to do anything to help the extraction along. I had never reached the place in my meditation practice of having conversations with my body, so this was a really hard assignment for me to wrap my head around. I tried several times, but I just couldn't do it. Finally, in an act of generosity and compassion, my therapist led me through a meditation to get started.

Phyllis was the name my fibroid chose for herself. At first, we asked her to absorb any negative energy that had settled in my body, taking on the grayness and leaving behind pink, healthy tissue. I sat with that for a few days, but it just didn't feel right to me—it felt selfish. I didn't want anything, not even an anomalous mass, to take on any of my burden. But as I became more comfortable with the notion of talking to Phyllis, I made an awkward attempt to re-engage in a conversation. It felt really odd at first, talking to a part of myself. Nonetheless, I proceeded.

As I spoke from my heart, the conversation began to soften and feel more natural, like two very caring friends lovingly holding each other. Instead of compromising herself and soaking up my bad stuff, I asked Phyllis to "take out the trash" on her way out. Then, given that she was made of uterine tissue and just about the size of a uterus at this point, I encouraged her to find a baby girl who was about to be born without one, just as I had been, and go be her uterus. It felt weirdly like I was telling her, "Fly, baby, fly," and yet it brought me so much peace.

As my surgery date drew closer, I noticed that I was getting a little scared, mostly about the pain. My therapist advised me to call on my angels to stand by my side and help me along the way. I started with the surgery site itself, my abdomen, and pictured the strongest women in my life sitting in a circle around it, holding hands and channeling their strength into my body. With that image alone, I started to feel stronger. I saw my soul sister holding my heart. I visualized my therapist on my shoulder, looking into my body, overseeing everything, ready to direct her magic inwardly wherever I needed it, while right beside her were my badass, no-nonsense girlfriends who would move mountains on the outside to make this surgery a success. All of a sudden, I no longer imagined myself alone on the operating bed—now all of my angels were with me.

When my surgery date arrived, Phyllis and I were ready, with my angels by my side. I was excited about the freedom that lay on the other side of the procedure for both of us. I was in tears thinking that, energetically anyway, perhaps because I had this fibroid, another girl would not have to endure the challenges that I have had to, being born without a uterus. And I was already shedding tears of gratitude for my angels who took the fear away. For me, it was a remarkable way to go into surgery, and it was really just a change in perspective.

I had the most wonderful post-op gift as well. For several weeks after my surgery, I did not have the strength to tuck my boys in bed as I used to. All three of us were desperate to find a solution, because it was a sacred time for us. Again showing their resilience and creativity, the boys dragged their sleeping bags into our bedroom and set up camp on the floor on either side of our bed. This led to night after night of entertaining bedtime "jam sessions" of stories from their infancy, "would you rather" discussions, and jokes, lots of jokes. Our new nighttime ritual has created the space for connection and memory-making in a way that I never would have dreamed of. Truly, necessity is the mother of *Remarkable Reinvention*!

Distant Connections

In addition to my day job as a marketing manager, I am also the *unofficial keeper of the soul of my team*. As such, I create opportunities and hold the space for each of my team members to grow individually, to strengthen as a group, and to develop as professionals. We cycle through these pillars each month during our weekly "Friday Power Hour." Since we collaborate across two states, pre-pandemic, our personal and professional learnings took place virtually whereas team building happened when we had the chance to meet in person. Our flights would bring us together from our respective cities and we would meet at a Starbucks for coffee, breakfast, and a catchup before heading into a day of customer meetings. We traversed company and industry events inseparably, tending to the business at hand and then enjoying a night on the town. We learned so much about each other during these excursions and became a strong support network for each other. We were a family with a bond that was palpable to anyone in our orbit. We were THE TEAM to be a part of and we all felt so blessed to be together.

When the pandemic hit and travel came to a screeching halt, it was a jolt for all of us. I, for certain, wasn't prepared to give up seeing my team once a month. Those get-togethers *were* the team-building pillar of our Friday Power Hours. I had to figure out how to pivot and strengthen our bond without traveling to be with each other. How do you deepen camaraderie virtually? How do you set the stage for on-demand connection, be it through fun and laughs or vulnerability and tears?

My team, like all teams in the company, in the country, on the planet, was faced with a huge obstacle to meaningful connection—distance. I had to make up for the lost hours of face-to-face time in which we shared our personal adventures. How? Through quality activities in mere one-hour increments that still offered the space for conversation to flow spontaneously. And so again, I got to work.

Our journey started very locally, with the team learning more about each other through happy hours and guided conversations about diversity and inclusion, as well as broader discussions using conversation-starter cards. It did not take long to realize that virtual happy hours can only go so far and their novelty can wear off quickly.

As I looked more closely at the deeper needs of our team, I came up with the topic of self-care. I could almost hear my teammates' gears turning when I introduced the topic, as if we were all realizing how much that had taken a back seat to the crisis at hand. It was fulfilling to offer ideas to help my team take care of themselves so that we could take care of each other. We expanded beyond ourselves for more self-care, inviting a guest speaker—the chiropractor wife of one of our teammates—to teach us how to stay safe ergonomically as we sat at our desks all day.

The bond continued to deepen as we looked at our personality profiles and how we all fit together, learning ways that we could work together even better. We were amused at the ahas, despite knowing so much about each other already. We even got together during one Team Friday Power Hour to give back to the broader community, sewing baby blankets for a hospital New Infant Care Unit. Where birthdays and milestones were once celebrated with a few words or a short text message, we were now having full-on party-paloozas with treats and props and games. We were connecting in ways we never had before, for reasons we never had before.

As I look back on how we reinvented our connections as a team, I am grateful for the opportunity, courage, and creativity to do it differently. When the world opens up and we get to hug each other in person, it will be that much sweeter.

What I've Learned

- Be present to your "now" and keep making it awesome.

The biggest realization I have had through these challenges is the fundamental truth that we only have today. Our present moment is all that is guaranteed. We must make the most of it, rather than taking the path of least resistance, settling for mediocrity, and waiting for things to improve later. I have learned that it is far more rewarding, on many levels, to make your own "awesome" proactively. And when it doesn't feel right to push for change, I've also learned to recognize that, so I can assess and pivot.

- We cannot fret and create at the same time, so fret fast and then create magic!

This was simultaneously my most volatile challenge *and* my most gratifying lesson. I noticed that when things did not go according to my plan or even went squarely against my plan, as long as I was upset about it, I could do nothing about it. Of course, it's okay to be upset—it's even natural and expected. So I would first sit with my frustration, anger, and disappointment. I'd feel it in my body. I journaled. I cried. I let it flow through me, and then it would exit my body—just like that. Then I was free to figure out a new path. The more quickly I dropped my resistance, the sooner I could feel the feelings and move on to create a solution.

- The solution may be as simple as a shift in perspective.

I didn't always have to move mountains or physically do *anything* in order to Reinvent my Remarkable. Oftentimes, I just had to reframe it, think about it differently, make it more of an inside job. Instead of focusing on what I did not like outside myself, I focused on what I wanted to feel inside. That revealed a new mantra and, with it, new hope.

- For certain, my road to Reinventing Remarkable will be paved with unexpected gifts.

This is the surprising and delightful gift for being committed to a Remarkable life. In having the courage to do things differently or try something altogether new, I am benefitting from perks that I never would have imagined when I was stuck in my old, comfortable way of doing things. In being ready, with eyes and heart wide open, I am able to recognize and appreciate the amazing and unforeseen gifts of nurturing my present.

How YOU Can Reinvent YOUR Remarkable

When you find yourself in the midst of a "now" that you don't like, here are a few steps you can take to recreate it so that it aligns with your desires:

1. Clear the path by feeling the feelings.

   You can't fret and create at the same time, so roll up your sleeves, dive in, and feel the feelings. It may be uncomfortable, so be gentle with yourself and know that you will come out on the other side with a lighter and brighter outlook.

2. Consider how you want to look back and remember your journey through this challenge.

   Take yourself many years into the future and reflect on the story you want to tell others about this time in your life. Note the thoughts, feelings, and actions that you want to recall from this time. Get clear about how you want your Remarkable Reinvention to look.

3. Plan your tactics to meet this challenge.

   Now it is time to chart your course. Think about what it will take to make your Remarkable come to life. You may include the actions you will take and the help you will ask for. You may add milestones for the journey and celebrations along the way.

4. Write down your plan . . . in pencil.

   Always listen for what is needed in the moment and be ready to change course.

5. Write a letter of gratitude . . . and read it . . . again and again.

Also known as writing a vision or "scripting," this step allows you to express your journey into existence. Take yourself into the future and imagine that you have made it through this challenge. Then write a letter of gratitude to whomever you envision supporting you on this journey. Express the joy in your heart, the peace in your soul, and any other emotions that come to mind. Read this letter often, even daily, to raise your spirits and set yourself on the path you envisioned.

Closing

This last year has presented me with the unique opportunity to Reinvent my Remarkable over and over again. I have shared the common themes, lessons, and steps that helped me pave this path and that delivered the delightful and unexpected gifts I have enjoyed along the way. My hope is that these stories and learnings will help you do the same when it is time for you to Reinvent YOUR Remarkable, too.

Ratika Hansen is mama to twin boys, a wife, and a marketing manager in the high-tech industry. She is also a long-standing student of personal growth, devoting the last twenty years of her life to learning from masters in the field and putting their lessons into practice. Her life purpose is to use what she learns on this journey to inspire passionate living in the hearts of the willing so we all bring our light to the world. Her own light shines most brightly as grace, ease, joy, inspiration, and love.

*As a two-time best-selling contributing author, certified Passion Test facilitator, and credentialed Make A Difference seminar leader, Ratika has shared her personal life shifts to inspire thousands of people to live passionate lives, bringing their light to their relationships, their careers, and their communities. Visit **ToYourPassionateLife.com** and **Facebook.com/ToYourPassionateLife** for gifts of inspiration to brighten your day.*

Unlocking Keys to Your Inner Clarity and Unique Voice
There are no wrong turns
by Debra Eklove

Setting Out

I remember the conversation clearly, as if it happened yesterday. I was sixteen years old, standing in a phone booth, talking to my dad, feeling confused and overwhelmed. My university admission form was due that week and I needed to make a decision: should I study music or commerce? My dad, a successful self-made businessman and a gifted singer, excelled in both. I trusted that his advice, based on extensive personal experience, would help me decide.

Have you ever been at a turning point in your life, unsure of which way to go? That was me, torn between choosing two very different directions.

I grew up in a loving, beautiful, and sheltered home. As the youngest of three, I had limited ideas of how the world worked and what I could contribute. I did know that I wanted to make people happy. From a young age, I spent my time at family gatherings circulating from room to room, eavesdropping on conversations like a fly on the wall, soaking in the latest gossip and stories from the day. Taking care of people was my key motivation, and I heard that attribute in the men's business talk. So in pursuing higher education, commerce felt like the natural choice—practical, logical, and helpful. As I was a tomboy, I had no problem going into what was then considered a male field. But in my final year of high school, an eye-opening alternative appeared.

Miss Macdonald walked noisily into the music classroom, wearing three-inch, black patent-leather heels that clacked on the floor. She tossed her long red hair, beamed a wonderful smile, and captivated the class. I was smitten. I'd never met a woman who embodied such pure excitement, encouraging boys and girls alike with warmth and liveliness. Fresh out of teachers' college, young and clear, so giving and creative, she radiated a dynamic presence that filled me with what I yearned for, joy and anticipation.

To soak in this as much as I could, I found myself volunteering to help Miss Macdonald whenever possible. I was inspired by my muse, learning the art of singing and the importance of grouping voices, planning rehearsals, and choosing songs. I shyly opened up, hesitant to share ideas for music, areas I'd never explored before. She encouraged me with thoughtful glances and warm smiles.

At the Christmas concert, with her morale-boosting support, I recruited and organized eight friends from the large Jewish population at the school. For the first time, Hanukkah was featured at this holiday concert. At the end of its first half, with our heartbeats pushing us forward, we four girls and four boys, dressed in matching black outfits with homemade red capes, filed to the center of the stage. I bowed to the audience, terrified, then faced my friends to conduct. As we shared our love for all to hear, I felt a surge of peace.

At the end of the concert, I went to Miss Macdonald with a gigantic bouquet of red, yellow, white, and orange flowers in my arms. In the moment before I gave them to her, our eyes locked, my speechless gratitude flowed, and the whole world disappeared.

I had found a true love in music, but my mind second-guessed itself. So I called the person who I trusted completely. When I put my dilemma before my dad, he answered without hesitation, "Do commerce. You can always do music later." Because he had always worked hard to support the family, his answer reflected his concerns and reinforced some of my doubts about pursuing music. Education at that stage in my life was to be an investment. I could pursue education for pleasure later. His answer sealed my decision.

This was a fateful moment for me, and I hope you will learn from my story as you make such critical choices in your own life. I see it not as a wrong choice, just a different path, teaching me some vital lessons I'll share with you in this chapter.

That fateful decision earned me a degree in commerce, which led to pursuing a master's degree in economics. A few months into study, I faltered, overwhelmed with anxiety about what I was doing. Rethinking my chosen area of study, I switched from international trade to the economics of education and health, a fledgling field of specialization that would get me entry into the education field, which I decided interested me much more than traditional economics. I was starting to glimpse and reclaim my heart's yearnings.

After studies, armed with good degrees, I had plenty of work. People often created projects or positions for me in research, industry, and education. Two business people—a banker and an executive in a shipping company—told me that if I ever need work, I should contact them. While I was happy to help with worthwhile projects, inside I often felt confused, thinking, "Why are they making these offers to me? I don't know anything."

After working for a while, I felt lost and sad. Since I'd always enjoyed studying, it seemed logical to continue my education, and I was hopeful that this change would uplift me. The day before my PhD orientation, however, my body refused to leave the house. Every cell rebelled, telling me that one more day of struggling to fit into this chosen direction was impossible.

Has this ever happened to you? An opportunity shows up, or maybe you create an opportunity, so you go ahead and embrace it. But then you discover it is not very fulfilling. Maybe you don't actually enjoy the task, or you're trying to fit in, or you're swayed by what others think you should be doing. You let someone else's priorities guide you, and you lose the connection to—and joy in—what really lights you up.

Maybe in the beginning, you feel this is what you want, that your choice meets your desire for fulfillment, contribution, challenge or excitement. Then, over time, anxiety, doubt, and fear creep in, sometimes so slowly you hardly notice them, till they knock you down. That's what happened to me. Now I know that when I've been clear about my priorities, I see how the best projects, like those described below, may start out with effort and difficulties, but commitment makes the long term meaningful and joyful.

Turning Point

My living room was all ready as I moved a chair and made an open space in the middle. Tova arrived wearing a flowing dress and a beautiful smile, easily setting up her portable massage table so I could enjoy the massage, a mid-day treat.

She was a visitor in town and we had met a week before. I felt drawn to her inner calm and her outer shimmer of clarity. In our laughter, I felt a unique connection. We talked of my having a massage, and I felt safe and welcomed.

Silently, thoroughly, and lovingly, her experienced, intuitive hands worked the muscles in my legs and back, and kneaded my hands, neck, and head. My mind began to uncoil and then relax. Sleep arrived. When Tova gently spoke my name and rocked me, I returned from afar. It was time to get up.

While we were sitting together over a cup of tea, she gently asked, "How was the massage?"

I said, "Great."

She thoughtfully looked at me, or through me, and then carefully said, "When I worked on your back where you are supposed to have a reflex, you had none."

All I could say was, "Oh?" as her words were a shocking jab, reverberating through my body, and confusing me. What did she mean? At the time, I still had patterns of putting my trust in others, not in myself, so I thought, *My body is ill. My body is rebelling from years of fear and unexpressed nervousness. Was I anxious and petrified, like stone, unmoving and rigid to avoid feeling pain?*

Little did I know that this afternoon set the stage for my mind, body, and spirit to unfurl together.

An inner voice that I had never paid much attention to grabbed me with passionate determination: "Explore. Explore." I did so with a vengeance. Deep-tissue body massage by Russian-trained professionals whose motive was "no pain, no gain" was a beginning. For a while it felt right, then it was like I was punishing myself. I felt only pain and emptiness, and I stopped that torturous treatment.

One morning, the agony exploded out of me. Pacing back and forth, scaring the cat, afraid my neighbors would hear me, but unable to stifle my inner pain, I wailed with a sound that erupted from my core. I laugh now as I see how dramatically I ran to the bookshelf, put my head down, and let the tears flow and flow, drenching my sleeve. Wasted, I looked up, and there facing me was *A Guide for the Perplexed*, by E. F. Schumacher. I knew his work as an economist and philosopher, so reading his teachings on faith and spirit ignited the awe that I was burning to express.

I'd bought the book about four years earlier and never opened it. But over the next thirty-six hours, I devoured it from cover to cover with a growing knowledge that, even though I felt lost, I was taken care of in ways beyond my comprehension. Again, I resolved to explore my mind-body connection, this time with faith, gentle devotion, and love.

Taking care of myself, I became engrossed in tai chi. I found Grace, my kind, strong, and gentle masseuse—or she found me. After three sessions, one chilly fall afternoon in the middle of her Swedish treatment, I burst into tears. A dam had burst.

After that, it became normal for me to burst into tears in the middle of a massage or well up with emotion at other times during the day. Grace's experience and wisdom carefully guided me through my skittishness and blocks. After two years of working together, she suggested more subtle work with shiatsu, an energy-medicine tool for deeper internal explorations. Then, after many years of shiatsu, my sensei said, "With your intensity and dedication, you need to study shiatsu."

Shyly, the quiet, determined voice inside agreed. Energy and alternative wellness tools excited me completely. As I studied the ancient healing tools and cultures of China, Japan, South America, and India, my awe and appreciation for Life grew by leaps and bounds. In shiatsu, I loved understanding the body's flows of energy and rhythms. Working with fellow students was a joy, creating a wordless connection among us that was both deep and comfortable. After the one-year program, the sensei encouraged me to continue for the next session: a teacher-in-training. I was hesitant, but his belief in my abilities swayed me. With family support I adjusted my schedule to continue the intense training program, making it a priority in my life.

Three months into the graduate program, my sensei's young new wife joined the classes and began teaching. I welcomed her into this warm enclave. She brought embroidered fabrics and fresh flowers into the dojo to beautify the space, and I smiled at her with appreciation. As the training became more intense, the energy in the studio became more erratic, demanding, and unclear. Where once I felt relaxed and secure, I now felt wary and uncomfortable.

After the December evaluations, my sensei took me aside and unexpectedly confronted me—he told me to stop energetically attacking his wife. In shock and fear, I wondered what my energy was doing. Attacking anyone was totally outside my values. I saw myself as welcoming and friendly. But my teacher saw differently. Again, that old inner pattern said, *What is wrong with me?* Confused, I became hesitant in class, seeking reassurance that wasn't coming. It was a terrifying ordeal.

Finally, things came to a head. The following February, in the middle of a group class, Sensei abruptly said, "Debra, stand up.

Come to the middle of the room." Shaking, I walked forward. Then and there he ordered me to leave. I went blank. Stunned and devastated, I could only comply. I gathered up my pillows and robe, and silently left the room.

As I look back now, I see that the Universe gives us these challenging opportunities to help us, providing insights, exits from dead ends and opening new directions for growth. At the time, I felt destroyed. But I've since learned that experiences of shock provide necessary insights and I see them like the postman delivering necessary mail—unexpected letters—some are love notes and some are bills.

Years later, I bumped into spunky, sweet Carla from the shiatsu school and found out that within four months of my exit, all the teachers-in-training were expelled by the sensei. When I was forced out, I thought I was the problem. Carla showed me that the issue wasn't what my "energy" was doing; rather, it was my tendency to put trust into what others projected instead of embracing my energy sensitivity.

Being thrown out of shiatsu school only strengthened my resolve to "fix myself." When the Body and Soul Energy Medicine School opened, I joined the four-year training program with twenty-eight other wonderful seekers. Over the years, we discovered the many ways energy is held, used, expressed, and perceived.

Books, exercises, presentations, and hands-on work nurtured me. Though the process was very difficult and aimed to take me outside my comfort zone, I felt inspired. My body and mind felt safe, and offered images, thoughts, and stories. A favorite image that blossomed over time was of a basket containing unmoving forms that become kittens, which then began to breathe and snuggle with each other. When they awakened from slumber, each roamed freely inside me, growing into sensuous, keen cats. Awakening from slumber, I learned to trust this wonderful sensation of mind, body, and spirit uniting, trusting the present moment, trusting how the Universe cares deeply for my highest good.

If there's one core principle I've learned from all these experiences, it's this: Trust the Universe. All that happens is ultimately for our good. You are able to do only that which the Universe allows you to do, for your highest good. Each experience, whether it feels good or not, is a gift when you have the senses and heart to explore it. I love the image of a boat in the middle of the ocean, and what I think of as the winds and storms are simply ways to move the boat, you, to shore, to home. Relaxing into this truth makes Life the great journey, the great play, that is You.

Turning Back to Music

Now I see that my dad was right, in ways that I never imagined. My first studies in economics gave me a background in business, with crucial tools for the administration and leadership roles I've had with organizations that are aligned with my passion to develop serenity, contentment, and happiness. And for much of my life, music has been a vital hobby, a way to meet people and share spiritual bonds through words and songs. Once in the background, it became front and center.

For decades, my love of music was nurtured by singing in choirs and small groups whenever I could. If, at the beginning of a rehearsal I was sad or upset, the music helped lift the heaviness and I'd leave beaming with joy and gratitude.

Then, to my surprise, new original songs started to come through me, as whole entities, as poems, as wordless melodies, as prayers. Songs came during quiet times—in meditation retreats, in sleep, and once when sitting at a stoplight! With this creativity flowing, I learned to speak to the Universe: "Thank you for giving me this joy. How can I share it?"

The tiny voice inside propelled me to record my songs and poems. Hesitantly, I went to meet Eddie Baltimore, a kind man and an accomplished performer, guitarist, and producer. His basement studio was like a funhouse, a maze of curtains and sound barriers that opened and closed. The production room was only big enough for two small chairs and the recording equipment.

In our first meeting we talked for a bit, and then he asked me to sing. I was in awe. He said he would work with me. First I prayed, then I smiled and began.

Each session after that, I'd sit in the recording booth, singing solo and laying down tracks, and then we'd create accompaniment as needed. His encouragement and expertise are gifts I cherish.

Partway through preparing the ten tracks, my mother's health failed, from a cancer she never told us she had. My throat closed in grief. I had no heart for singing. I felt the need to retreat, but I could not leave my dad at this tender time. This is when I heard the Universe's tender and specific gift calling to me, through my friend Cathy. "You know, the Art of Living program I mentioned to you—meditation with yoga, and most importantly healing breathwork called Sudarshan Kriya, SKY? It's a weekend retreat, around the corner from your home, and offered at a student rate."

For me, it was the Universe divinely knocking, loud and clear, to change my direction. I now teach the Art of Living programs, helping others to reduce stress and open to happiness just as I was helped.

The SKY breath meditation program helped me calm my mind and overcome the grief, and time did its work. A year later, I wanted to finish the music I started.

But how? What to do? How to share these songs? My heart urged me to speak with the founder of the Art of Living, Gurudev Sri Sri Ravi Shankar, who was to speak nearby. I had met him once briefly, in a crowded room, at a July full-moon festival. In his gaze, I felt love and full. Gurudev always tells people, "There are no problems, but if you find any, bring your problems to me."

Now, sitting with thousands of people, soaking in his message, I didn't mind not understanding a word of Hindi. The message was heart to heart. But when he finished speaking and the crowd moved to leave, for a moment I panicked, wondering what to do. I took a breath and felt compelled to stay, and I silently joined a few others as we slowly walked away from the exits to a back room. There, watching as Gurudev sat with the event's organizers, his presence was palpable, and I felt such joy as each person he spoke to lit up from within. When he got up to leave, we all stood and as he passed in front of me, he stopped, with a big beautiful smile just for me. Stammering, I searched for something to say to this warmth and I blurted out, "I have some music to share." My CD, titled *A Process to Heart*, was completed at that moment and came into being four months later.

I have volunteered with the Art of Living in many capacities, as a singer, teacher, president of the Canadian organization, and now as a member of its board of directors. The mission of the foundation is creating a stress-free, violence-free society. Meditation, SKY breath, yoga, and Ayurveda (an Indian term meaning "The Science of Life") are ancient tools that are relevant for our modern life. Everyone can use these for a clear mind and body, to reduce stress and increase happiness.

My studies and work in industry, nonprofits, education, and health have all contributed to support this work. Singing in groups, or "sangha," as it is called, is a crucial part of staying balanced and happy. Through all the twists and turns in my life, I was guided to this unexpected and fulfilling life focus, allowing me to use all the tools and experiences I have gathered and be of service to fulfill a mission of peace for the world. Everything that I've done has brought me, step by step, to a place I could never have imagined, a place that has allowed me to trust my gifts and to embrace my childhood dream—to make people happy.

Anger, frustration, uncertainty, and anxiety still happen. Emotions like these are the human condition. I have learned to accept them without avoiding or minimizing them. They are cues and keys to learning and growing. Now I focus on where I am and what I can do for the highest good and the best outcomes.

And that's what I want for you. Let me share a few of the lessons I've learned so you too can experience the joy of relaxing into Life. Let's begin with a story.

With preparations for moving underway, the garage filled up with boxes. On moving day, as I opened the garage door to bring out another box, I saw the bird. She was desperately throwing herself against the closed window at the back of the garage. I thought, "If only the bird would turn around to see where I was standing, she'd see the doorway behind me open." Scanning the room, I spied a broom and grabbed it. I climbed around a few boxes to reach the bird and gently swung at her. At first she fluttered in fear, then turned, and seeing the sunlight, dashed out to her next adventure.

I laughed. The bird mirrored me. So many times in my strong-minded determination, I have charged ahead—in the wrong direction. Thankfully, there have been people and events in my Life with "brooms" to set me straight. What may have seemed scary at the time was only there as a gift to help me turn and fly into the direction of light and joy.

Here's what I hope you will take away from this chapter. Changing habits takes time, and I suggest you implement what you can in baby steps, starting with what feels the best for you . . .

Lesson #1

There really are no wrong turns. Through all the trips, programs, projects, advice, and detours in my life, I've discovered each has its purpose and value. For me, the plan in my head, the programming of my youth, and the choices I'd seen friends make were so different from how my life evolved. Social conventions shaped me so strongly that I suppressed my fears and anger, contracted my energy, disconnected my mind from my spirit and body, and looked to others for what I needed to do and be, wanting to please everyone.

Until I learned to change my judgments from "This is bad" and "I don't want this" to "This is teaching me something important" and "This is what I truly need," I beat myself up. Even feeling deep anxiety and fear, I learned to embrace new paths and delight in the appreciation, wonder, and awe that now illuminate my life. You can do that, too. You too can see how the twists and turns in your life are actually gifts for you to appreciate and unwrap, layer by layer.

For example, studying economics and traveling gave me insights into the diversity and complexity of our world. Teaching

Ayurveda, yoga, meditation, and breathwork have given me an appreciation for the journey from disharmony to harmony, from chaos to bliss. Singing and writing music have grounded my soul in vibrations of grateful liberation. Service in international humanitarian and charitable organizations has inspired me and is an outlet to work for the highest good.

Lesson #2

"The past is destiny. The future is free will." This quote from Gurudev Sri Sri Ravi Shankar, founder of the Art of Living Foundation, is Life changing. What happened in the past took you to this present moment. Your thoughts, desires, and decisions in the present moment set your course for the future. The Universe co-creates with you, providing the best outcomes for the time. Co-creation. What you ask for, the Universe provides.

Trust in the Universe can take time, overcoming the many voices giving advice and the many energetic currents rushing and pushing at you. Co-creating with the Universe means being open to what is offered in this present moment, asking for what you want, and trusting your inner voice with small and large issues.

One wintry cold Friday, when all I wanted to do was curl up with a cozy blanket, I had an unexplainable urge to go to the promotional program of the home water-filtration system that I sold, even though I didn't have a new person to bring. It became a bit of an obsession, which surprised me, but by then I had learned to listen to my inner voice. I knew something unique would happen, and it did. I won the raffle that night for a complete portable system.

Another time, needing extra income to help pay expenses, a thought came as a question: "What could I do?" The next day, a friend called to ask if I could take over her contract for $5,000, the exact amount I wanted, by managing a trade show. Having asked and received, I said, "Universe, thank you, more, please." The present moment is not a point on a line. The present contains all that is here—past, present, and future. The present is deep, wide, and vast and you have infinite possibilities within you to co-create with the Universe. I like to think of the present as the field of all possibilities, the place in which we can open up to the best outcomes, our highest good.

Lesson #3
Have faith in three areas:

- First, have faith in your process. It's where you were born, your gender, your education, your career, and relationships. Look at what you are going through as your process, as tools to learn from and use.

- Second, have faith in your teachers, mentors, and leaders. Honor your parents and people who gave you advice that benefited your life.

- And third, most importantly, have faith in yourself. You can overcome all obstacles. Have faith and trust this unchanging you, the inner voice of your spirit—this place untainted, uncheated, unabandoned, and always present for your greatest good. It's a special voice that comes in quiet times as your advocate, your cheerleader.

If you haven't already welcomed this part of you, are you wondering, *How do I access my true self?* To start, take baby steps.

Whenever you look in a mirror, stare straight and say, "Wow. That is the most wonderful person in the mirror. Wow." How do I know this? The Universe has you here, as simple as that. No one else is you in the body and mind that is you. Take a moment to notice one feature that draws your attention—your smile, your freckles, a curve, your wrist. Each day, find another part of you to love, bit by bit. You can go beyond noticing your physical attributes and move to noticing the sparkle in your eyes, the lift of your chest, a feeling of contentment, even sadness. You are much, much bigger than what you see.

The future is unknown. So be positive with Trust and Faith that you are able and capable, that you are taken care of, and that your skillful actions, thoughts, and speech all work to create the best.

Doubt saps our energy by keeping the mind in the past asking why, which is a futile question. "Who am I?" is a better question, because it allows you to get to a place of wonder. The question is more important than the answer.

Having Faith in yourself includes listening to your own inner voice. Often it is a small voice that whispers to you from inside, a place of silence and stillness at the heart of your being. Anchor in its infinite peace. Looking back, I see how being open and receptive to my inner voice moved me away from a path I felt obligated to follow toward one that truly lights me up from the inside out.

As Steven Jobs said, you can't connect the dots going forward, but you can when you look backwards. Each turn can give you tools, strength, curiosity, and courage to compose a most beautiful life, fulfilling dreams beyond your imagination.

Lesson #4

Accept that everything changes. You have very little control except to allow yourself to move from misery toward happiness. This requires letting go when you are truly miserable, whether it's because of a job, a relationship, or a failed plan. Sometimes the need to let go is obvious. Sometimes it's not, but you have to acknowledge that you want a change. Sometimes you hold on because you are afraid or stuck.

Transformational leader Debra Poneman reminds us of Aristotle's phrase: "Nature abhors a vacuum." In order to create a vacuum and attract what you want, you need to let go of whatever is in the way. Letting go shows trust, and the Universe rewards this courage.

Here are some questions Debra suggests you ask to find out whether it's time to let go and make space for something new:

Do I feel respected and heard? Or do I feel resentful and compromised?

Do I feel peaceful? Do I feel exhausted, emotionally, spiritually, or physically?

Am I growing and pursuing my cherished goals?

Am I having fun? Am I truly me, or someone I hardly recognize?

Lesson #5

You can change your emotions and your mind with your breath. Every emotion has a different breathing pattern. Do you notice that when you are angry, your breath becomes hot, shallow, and fast? How do you breathe when you are surprised? You stop!

While breath patterns change with your emotions, you can learn to have your breathing patterns change your emotions. Observe every in breath and every out breath. Without breath, where would you be? Your breath is an amazing key to life, and when you honor and respect it, and use it as a tool, magic happens. Worldwide, the SKY breath meditation, a rhythmic breathing process, uses the breath to reduce stress and change emotions. SKY stands for Sudarshan Kriya, Sanskrit words: *Su* means "proper," *darshan* means "vision," and *kriya* is "a joyful action." Through the joyful action of this SKY breath, you obtain a proper vision of Life as it is. I have practiced this for almost twenty years. As a teacher of SKY breath, I have seen frowns turn to smiles, anxious people relax, and stress replaced by confidence and resilience.

Because you breathe only in the present, awareness of the breath keeps you in the present. Simple, yes? Even when you remember past events, you are remembering them in the present moment. When you plan or get excited about future events, you do it in the present. Only in the present do you decide what actions to take, what speech to verbalize, and which thoughts to keep. In the present are all possibilities.

Only in the present do you experience touch, smell, sight, taste, or sound—experiences we name as pleasant or unpleasant, happy or unhappy. If you think about it, happiness does not lie in the tasty candy, the fancy watch, or the delightful music. Happiness is the way those things make us feel. They only trigger the happiness that is inside us.

Reading the ancient scriptures that describe the science of yoga, the Yoga Sutras of Patañjali (*sutra* means "verse"), and practicing Sri Sri Yoga and Sri Sri Ayurveda, I have learned how the body and mind need to work together, to be flexible and expansive, for Life energy to flow. The ancient sage named Patañjali scientifically describes the impacts of cravings and aversions. He shows how when we don't crave happiness, we are free, in the present moment. When we don't crave even freedom, we obtain everlasting, unchanging, untainted Love.

Lesson #6

If you want only one central key, it is Gratitude. Research shows many health benefits of gratitude, such as increased immunity, reduced anxiety and depression, improved sleep, and reduced pain. Gratitude is truly an attitude to be developed. Having faith, staying in the present, and using the breath to let go of misery are all paths for bringing more gratitude into your life.

When grateful, you say thank you. When grateful, you appreciate what is and what changes. When grateful, you see ways to do acts of kindness. When grateful, you can be at peace.

Keep a gratitude journal and before sleep each day, write down three things for which you are grateful: for waking up, for a roof, for food, for people, or for things and events big and small. When you imagine how these would impact you were they lacking, gratitude can multiply.

When grateful, your appreciation co-creates with the ever-present eternal consciousness of the Universe and sets the stage for the Universe to give more appreciation. When something good happens say, "Thank you and may I have more." When something else happens say, "Thank you, may this obstacle or setback teach me well for my best outcome."

When you get to a stage where you are grateful for everything, judgments of both good and bad fall away. There you see life, with awe, wonder, and appreciation. Grateful for what is, for breath, you have the freedom to be yourself, to be joyful, and to be living in the present.

Feel gratitude for our very existence, our very body,
all that we have and all the love we have received.
And this gratefulness will bring you a flood
of prosperity, joy and happiness.

Gurudev Sri Sri Ravi Shankar

"Awe"

Can you allow the rain?
Can you let the sun shine?
Can you surrender to the fading flowers?

Can you watch the wind?
Can you allow thirst?
Can you let the hands warm?
Can you surrender to skin flaking off?
Can you watch a sigh?

All the same. A masterful plan mirrors everywhere.

Can you allow tears?
Can you let anger rise?
Can you surrender to loss?
Can you watch longing?

What is their name?
Water, Fire, Earth, Wind in Space create ripples and sensations.
Observe them. Inside and out. Then let them go.

All there is: Awareness to Witness and Experience.
AWE

Debra Joy Eklove is a healer, teacher, and intuitive musician. She is grateful to be able to dedicate her life to helping the lives and welfare of others. Starting out as an economist, for twenty-five years she worked in industry and managed not-for-profit organizations. A shocking event redirected her career to exploring and focusing on the importance of mind, body, and spiritual connections for wellbeing and health. She trained as a shiatsu and an energy medicine practitioner and had a successful private practice with hands-on healing modalities.

A gifted singer and intuitive musician, her CD called A Process to Heart *combines her love of devotional music and healing. She offers unique personal growth programs and individual sessions that include sound as therapy and vibrational awareness through song.*

*Debra is currently a teacher with the Art of Living Foundation, a volunteer-based international organization dedicated to bringing peace to the world, one person at a time. She is a sought-after mentor and teacher for meditation, SKY Breath, Sri Sri Yoga, and Ayurveda. Connect with her at **debrajoyeklove.ca**.*

Whether You Are 16 or 96,
It's Never Too Late to Be Happy

by Doris Slongo

Whew, *that one made it! Nick has gone ... Lucky him!* I'm standing on a little green hill next to my schoolhouse on a cold December day. The news of Nick's suicide hits me to the core. He was thirteen years old.

I feel for him. I feel connected to him, even though I didn't know him personally. He was a student from another class at my school.

I hear from his classmates that he decided to play with his longed-for electric train in heaven since he couldn't get it from his parents for Christmas. His grades at school turned out to be lower than the condition his parents had set for him to get the big Christmas present.

How good it must be where he is now, I think. *How light, how free he must feel.*

I feel a longing to be so free and careless too, away from this life down here, away from the daily strain at home. I feel I can't stand it any longer.

The school bell rings. It calls the laughing and playing children and me back to our classrooms.

·· ◆ ◆ ◆ ◆ ◆ ··

"Your skirts are of no value, only dead losses!" my father shouts at my mother and me. Again. My mother and I retreat to the kitchen as a place of relative safety. Some days ago, he yelled at me and then beat me with our dog's leather leash. He was angry since I hadn't followed his command immediately.

Sometimes I perceive some softness in him toward me. This is when he takes me aside and enjoys my female body. "Don't tell anything to Mommy because this would make her very sad, okay?" he says. I promise not to say anything.

My mother is the only love and support I have. Through her delicate face and her light blue eyes, I can feel her angelic nature. This is where I find my home—she is the ground on which I stand. Her eyes are deeply sad. Of course, I will not tell her anything.

My father is full of negativity. He treats those around him accordingly—his family, neighbors, and friends. Friends? He has no real friends.

My mother's social contacts are limited to a few neighbors and two friends from her youth, with whom she talks on the phone from time to time. My father would not tolerate more. She's always at home, except when she needs to go to town to buy family necessities. She feels isolated, making her all the more vulnerable to my father's moods. Sometimes bluish bumps on her forehead or elsewhere on her body tell me stories of his violence. She tries to hide what she is going through, but I feel more than eyes can see.

My sister and I are lucky enough to be able to escape for a few hours when we go to school in the morning and afternoon. At lunch and in the evenings, when my father is always at home, tensions and terror are omnipresent.

I hear people say that childhood is carefree and cheerful and that after childhood, life becomes more difficult and demanding. *Even more difficult, even harder...?* I ask myself. *So that means the older I grow, the worse life will become?*

No, never. I cannot imagine bearing even more of the heaviness that already resides inside me. Life would finally become pitch black and there would be no more sunshine, no more butterflies, and one day no more consoling mother.

What's the point of living? I think.

I am deeply sad and I have been feeling this way for so long, as long as I can remember. There is nobody I can talk to about all of this. My mother is already suffering tremendously herself, and telling her how I'm really feeling would massively increase her pain and sadness. And her pain is my pain too.

I feel exhausted. I am thirteen years old. I have no more strength. I am chronically tense. My breathing has become constantly shallow. I cannot see clearly anymore. I am longing for salvation.

Fast Forward to the Present

Today I am happy. I am grateful for all that I had to go through. As a child, I didn't know that every pain, every struggle, and every disgusting life condition that I endured would make me a stronger and braver person in the future. But during those moments of pain and despair, it was hard to recognize the gifts that were hidden within them.

By not evading the pain, and instead confronting what hurt me and enduring it, I experienced that my pain didn't kill me— it gradually became lighter and more bearable. It transformed. Eventually, some light appeared, leading me to suspect that I was growing out of this darkness into the morning of a new and positive *joie de vivre*.

Life gradually gifted me with such transformation of pain into a growing source of strength that it set free my strong, innate zest for life.

This is the alchemy that is set in motion when we face the pain, accept it, and endure it, trusting that our suffering will transform and a new path will reveal itself.

I think this is what the mystic Rumi meant eight hundred years ago when a disciple asked him how to deal with the suffering and pain in his heart. "Stay with it," he answered. "The wound is the place where the light will enter you."

My conscious journey to discover innate happiness began years after the painful time of my youth. When I was sixteen years old, the mother of my friend Marietta gave me a book. Marietta and her family were neighbors in our apartment building. Marietta's mother, Mrs. Lapp, happened to notice my mother sitting alone on the balcony, crying. Mrs. Lapp went over to my mother to comfort her. When I visited Marietta's family shortly thereafter, I told them about the difficulties in our everyday life. Mrs. Lapp then gave me a book and said that it would certainly help me and my mother.

This book became the starting point of my own life, one in which I became inwardly free from the paralyzing sadness and grueling tensions that constantly lay over my home and burdened me deeply.

Decades later, I still have that book: *How to Stop Worrying and Start Living* by Dale Carnegie. It taught me how to interpret daily life differently so that it no longer weighed on me as much. Carnegie emphasizes that our thoughts determine our life and that we can easily change our experience through positive thinking. He says, "The biggest problem you will face . . . is choosing the right thoughts."

Carnegie cites the French philosopher Michel de Montaigne, who said, "A person is hurt not so much by what is happening as by his opinion about it." Carnegie showed me how to focus on the bright side of life and how to let go of the things that cannot be changed at the moment. In the years that followed, I often said to my mother, "Just look at the good things in your life. Please stop worrying. You can always deal with the problems later. If you then still need to face them, they will be a lot smaller." Carnegie's book started me on the path of a joyful, lifelong journey filled with countless books, CDs, workshops, and seminars on broader horizons in life and its wider contexts—insights that I was never taught in school. Over time, what I learned set me free. My way to inner freedom and happiness was also shaped by my own experiences, the ones that all of us get served in everyday life, and my insights from life's lessons.

Here are some of the cornerstones of my personal journey to happiness.

Create Islands of Happiness for Mental Balance

I hope that my experience will help you move through whatever challenges you may be facing in your life. So let me share some of the key lessons I've learned in hopes you will find them useful.

Intuitively, in my childhood and teenage years, I was looking for balance in my stressful home. As much as possible, I escaped outside to play with the kids in the neighborhood, and every Saturday I went to Girl Scout meetings. These activities were oxygen for my soul.

School was a refuge for me, too—it was a safe place where I felt secure. I was fully present there, so learning was easy and a pleasure for me.

When I was fourteen, I was allowed to take my first dance lessons. How I loved them! Whenever another class was offered, I took it. Later, ballroom dancing became my passionate hobby. Several times a week my dance partner, Peter, and I trained together with other couples in the dance club. On weekends we often participated in tournaments all over the country. Or we would go dancing somewhere, in clubs and at village festivals (where dancing was the most fun). My life was filled with school and dance training, dance events, and tournaments for the Swiss championship (I lived in Switzerland then and now), giving me hours of happiness.

Still, I had to endure the other ten hours of the day at home, where I tried to support my beloved mother. I was so grateful to her for paying our English dance coach, who gave us a private lesson every week. My mother saved that money from her already meager household budget. She had to account for her purchases every month to my father, but she somehow managed to hide the money for our dance coach among the expenses. My mother was my hero.

My outside activities were windows to my innate love of life, and gradually my heart became lighter. These islands of happiness strengthened me and made it possible for me to endure the hardships that remained in my life.

Fortunately, I did come in contact with families in which life was beautiful, loving, and joyful. There was the family of my first boyfriend, Eddy. For the first time in my life, I experienced a family atmosphere that was harmonious and loving. I almost couldn't believe that this existed! Parents who treated each other very affectionately and cordially? Was that real? Or a fiction? It was real. Eddy's parents understood and respected each other, and they were happy, yes, really happy together.

Wow, this really exists! I thought. How lucky and grateful I felt to experience heaven on earth between two people. Witnessing this kind of relationship was a revelation to me. I took it as a gift and a guiding star for my future, nourishing my soul with this ideal image of a harmonious relationship and family life. *This will be possible for me as well,* I thought. I was seventeen years old when I made this conscious decision. It was my secret pact with the Universe; only the Universe and I knew about it.

Choose to Be Happy!

Happiness is a choice.

This may sound absurd to you. You might be thinking, *People say I should choose to be happy. How is that possible when so many things in my life are not the way I want them to be? I have far too little reason to be happy!* Some people think that you cannot choose happiness. There is even some research that says that you can influence your own happiness by only 40 percent, because 50 percent is genetically determined and 10 percent is environmentally dependent. I don't agree with this at all. My personal experience shows that you can be happy in spite of your genes.

My parents were anything but happy, and my childhood memories show the picture of unhappy grandparents. According to the research mentioned above, I could never have become truly happy. But the opposite is true. I increasingly found ways to become deeply happy and grateful—because I decided to.

The phrase "choose to be happy" means that you can step out of your habitual and often unconscious twilight state of only half happiness or moderate contentment or even misery and feel brighter, more hopeful, kinder, and more joyful. You can say to yourself, "Life will provide solutions, I am hopeful" or even "I feel happy now." By doing this, you will immediately feel lighter. Your heart will open up, you'll find reasons for a more positive perspective, and you'll feel a little more cheerful. As soon as you tell yourself that you feel happier, ideas will spontaneously arise that make you feel even brighter. Then act from your improved state of contentment, and happier moments will line up. Give it a try!

If the leap from your current inner state to feeling happy seems too big, then simply decide to feel a bit better. For example, if you feel restless, imagine what it would be like to feel calm. You will immediately breathe deeper, and your facial and body muscles will relax. You can then go further if you like, for example, by choosing to feel hope. By doing so, you will start seeing views and possibilities that give reasons for hope. Now act from this mental attitude. Experience how it exhilarates you. Life will then show you more reasons to feel good. Allow some joy to arise. Stay with it. It will increase.

One of the most important lessons on my journey was to forgive my father instead of hating and blaming him for my suffering and that of my mother. True, we were at his mercy, and he was the cause of our pain and depression. *But what if,* I asked myself, *he was only an involuntary actor on this stage of life?* Over the years, many conversations and books have led me to understand how my father was shaped by his childhood and how his behavior was the result of those experiences. I understood that each person does their best with what is possible for them in each situation. Nobody chooses voluntarily and consciously to be nasty, cruel, or even criminal. Actions are always based on past (and mostly unconscious) negative conditioning and experiences.

I came to understand this even more deeply and convincingly many years later as an attorney-at-law dealing with offenders. The people I visited in prison in preparation for trial were limited in their abilities to live their lives correctly and successfully. Their personalities had been deeply disturbed in childhood, and they did not choose the crimes they committed fully voluntarily. This does not mean that society should tolerate crimes, because offenders must be resocialized, if possible, and society must be protected from further criminal acts. But due to those clients and my defense work, I learned a lot about human nature.

Forgive, Forgive, and Forgive

My father's personality was characterized by a need to destructively exert power over others. I understood over the years that he felt frustrated, and he compensated for his sense of powerlessness by dominating and tormenting those who were closest to him and who were at his mercy. His personality was too undeveloped and immature to recognize what was going on, so he wasn't able to moderate himself. His parents could not give him a foundation of love and from his childhood he carried unhealed injuries into his adulthood.

In those days, it was unknown or frowned upon to heal oneself internally with the help of psychotherapy and to develop one's own loving personality. "Men are strong and have no psychological problems" was his mantra. It was engraved in each of his cells. He didn't have the broader horizon to recognize and work on the dysfunctions in his personality in order to become a content, loving husband and father.

From this point of view, I recognized my father as a victim of his own history, and this gave me a new understanding of his actions toward us. The insight that he didn't know better eventually enabled me to forgive him.

Did my forgiving justify his actions toward us? No, they remained the wrongs that they were. Forgiving is not approving what has happened. Forgiving is a gift that the forgiver gives to themself. By being able to forgive, you redeem yourself from the resentment that sits within you. By forgiving, you let go of that grudge against the other person or the circumstances that so tormented you. By doing so, you don't undo what happened, but you free yourself from the poisons of hatred, revenge, frustration, or other negative feelings that otherwise would continue to reside within you and decimate your enjoyment of life, whether consciously or unconsciously.

Step Out of Your Old Shoes

What are your past roles that you would like to step out of?

For a while, I made a joke of being especially loving toward my father despite his rude behavior. I stepped out of the familiar pattern of the inferior victim and played a new role. I played this role consciously, like in a play. I felt invulnerable. In those moments, I was no longer his victim and he could no longer act in his usual role.

This made my father vulnerable because he was confused. He couldn't interpret what was going on. That was wonderful! Now

I was dominating the game. Not with his rules of aggression and contempt, but with my rules of friendship and unconditional love. This unfamiliar experience disarmed him.

Once I visited my parents and brought my father some flowers that I had picked by the wayside. Usually, I brought flowers for my mother. This time, however, I gave them to my father with a smile: "For you, Daddy." He was amazed and speechless. I gave him the flowers as if it were something natural in our family, not expecting any thanks. I did not wait for his reaction but turned to other things. I celebrated for myself, knowing that I was untouchable and he was unable to launch his usual attacks.

With my unexpected and loving actions, I became an active shaper of the relationship. In such moments I no longer played the old game of the tortured victim. Without his usual victim, my father could not play that game either. He had to leave his ingrained patterns behind.

These experiences and similar ones in later life taught me what a blessing it can be to take a leap forward and leave old dynamics behind.

Be Consciously Grateful on a Daily Basis

Through many personal experiences, I learned how valuable and important it is to be grateful for the good things in life and to consciously appreciate them.

Look around you. Can you be grateful that you have shelter to protect you from wind and rain? Can you be thankful that you have enough to eat and drink today? Can you be thankful that you have a friend? Can you be thankful that you woke up this morning with your heart still beating? Can you be thankful that you got to go to school? Can you be thankful that you have a job or an occupation that inspires you? Can you be grateful that you live in a country where there is minimal threat to your security? Can you be grateful that you are able to read and understand this book that you hold in your hands, and that your mind and heart are open to learn from it?

I'm sure at least a few of these things apply to you, if not all. Can you give a loving YES to some of these questions and feel gratitude in your heart? Linger with it. Can you feel new energy arising in you that fulfills and satisfies you?

I often reflect on the things that are good in my life. And without exception, I always feel the great power that bubbles up when I am consciously grateful. Being consciously grateful became the most important tool for me to be quickly and deeply satisfied. And such deeply felt gratitude is already halfway to happiness.

Consider the little things you can be grateful for in life. Write them down in a notebook. Then in the evening or the next day, reflect on more reasons you can be grateful, or rewrite what you've been grateful for in the past. Every time you do that, it sinks deeper into the subconscious. Take some time to dwell on each point of gratitude and feel gratitude flowing through you and bubbling up within you. Feel how beneficial this is.

Get in Touch with Your Inner Child

Along my path, I also learned about working with my inner child. My pottery and painting teacher was also a therapist, and she taught me that we are never alone, but always together with our inner child.

We think we are alone, a single self, but in fact we all carry our inner child with us all the time. I have been fortunate enough to learn to perceive my inner child, an inner voice that comes forward when I turn within and cautiously tap on her door.

In the beginning, when you are not yet used to talking to your inner child, there may seem to be nothing there. It takes some patience until it starts to answer because it's not used to being asked how it feels, what it needs, and what we can do for it. Your inner child is comparable to your physical heart. Most of us are not consciously aware of it, but as soon as we turn to our heart, we feel our heartbeat and whether or not our heart is tense. The nonphysical level of the heart is what we perceive as emotions. We feel there, for example, whether we are sad or happy. Your inner child resides there.

The best thing to do is take a notebook and start writing down a dialogue with your inner child. It's amazing what it has to say to you. The more familiar it becomes with being noticed and with you listening to it, the more it opens up. It tells you about truths that lie hidden deep within you. Sometimes it lets you know that it needs protection, sometimes guidance, sometimes comfort, and sometimes more joy. Often it simply needs to be perceived, to be understood. It needs you to make it feel that someone cares for it. Healing begins and a new life force awakens.

When you visit your inner child often, it also tells you what it needs in order to be happy. It is very intelligent and creative, and it is honest. It is a precious guide for a happier and more fulfilling life.

Make Conscious Decisions to Be Happy, Every Day

We are each born with a great potential for happiness. Let's look at newborn babies. They are deeply happy from the inside out.

Our innate potential for happiness has often been bottled up by experiences that led to fear, sadness, and anger. As a result, we feel restless, exhausted, and sometimes even depressed. We feel that we are not happy, not really fulfilled in life.

Because we've gotten used to this state, perhaps over years or decades, it becomes the familiar water in which we swim. Only when the level of restlessness, exhaustion, or depression becomes so strong that, for example, we show physical symptoms or our relationships fall apart do we become aware of how the life we lead is destructive and makes us unhappy.

We then think that we need to change the external circumstances in order to feel better. This can certainly help. However, it is more important that we know that our true happiness always lies within and that our true happiness can only grow from within.

Whether you're 16 or 96, it's never too late to uncover the potential for happiness that lies hidden within you and to become really happy.

Here's the good news: you can decide for yourself whether and to what extent you want to uncover the innate happiness that is independent of external circumstances.

There are times in our lives when we wake up from lethargy and resignation and become aware that we are not living our full happiness potential because too much fear or sadness paralyzes us. These are moments when we consciously long to step out of this morass of negative feelings and take a step toward a freer and happier life. We long for our own inner happiness to grow and expand. In such moments, the dark clouds give way to the sky and we can take significant steps toward becoming happy.

Your time for this has come. It is here and NOW.

If not now, when? Don't put off being happy. We have all learned from our experiences that we cheat ourselves out of true happiness when we put it off until later. Do you want to be happy only when the circumstances in your life have changed? When you have found your great love, when you can go on vacation, when the weekend has come, when you have your ideal body shape, when you earn more money, when . . . ? The list is endless if you don't decide to be happy right now.

Something surprising will happen if you decide to be happy from now on. You will succeed increasingly in being happy without external conditions, from within yourself. As a result, changes will magically happen in your life that increase your happiness without having to make any conscious effort.

Are you willing to give it a try?

Some Pills from the Happiness Medicine Cabinet

Try out some of these suggestions.

- Find islands of happiness for your mental equilibrium with activities you enjoy.

- Forgive, again and again, yourself and others, so that you can let go of the heavy burdens of negative feelings and thus feel lighter.

- Step out of your old shoes. Try new ways of looking at life.

- Be consciously grateful on a daily basis for all that is good in your life.

- Get in touch with your inner child. Write down dialogues with it.

- Make conscious decisions every day to be happy.

Take these pills from today on. Take your first step now, in this moment . . . and stay tuned.

Some of the Guides along My Journey

Here are some guides I have enjoyed along my journey that you may also find helpful.

- Brandon Bays, *The Journey*
- Robert Betz, *Step Out of Your Old Shoes*
- Gregg Braden, *The Spontaneous Healing of Belief*
- Dale Carnegie, *How to Stop Worrying and Start Living*
- Paolo Coelho, *Manual of the Warrior of the Light*
- Mihaly Csikszentmihalyi, *Flow*
- Ruediger Dahlke, *The Healing Power of Illness*
- Thorwald Dethlefsen, *Challenge of Fate*
- Wayne Dyer, *There's a Spiritual Solution to Every Problem*
- Shakti Gawain, *Creative Visualization*
- Neville Goddard, *The Power of Awareness*
- Bruce Lipton, *The Biology of Belief*
- Dan Millman, *Way of the Peaceful Warrior*
- Joseph Murphy, *The Power of Your Subconscious Mind*
- Margaret Paul and Erika J. Chopich, *Healing Your Aloneness*
- Norman Vincent Peale, *The Power of Positive Thinking*
- Catherine Ponder, *The Dynamic Laws of Prosperity*
- Anthony Robbins, *Awaken the Giant Within*
- Don Miguel Ruiz, *The Four Agreements*
- Eckhart Tolle, *The Power of Now*
- and many others.

Doris Slongo *made a decades-long impressive learning journey of personal and professional growth and has been sharing knowledge and wisdom from her experiences. She holds a doctorate in law and a master's degree in International Business Law. As an attorney-at-law in Zurich, she is committed to finding win-win conflict resolutions for her clients and advises companies and individuals on strategic and legal issues; she also supports them as a personal coach. She taught at the University of Zurich for twenty years and became known for her many years of legal advice to the public on Swiss radio and television. Parallel to her professional path, she overcame major hurdles in her private life. At the age of sixteen, she transformed from a teenager previously depressed by family circumstances into a happy, radiant, and successful woman. Besides her activities as a lawyer and a coach she is currently working on her new book with the working title "A Plea for Happiness." She can be reached at* **contact@dorisslongo.ch**

Your BIG IDEA Is Inside You
by Kay McDonald

Have you ever had a great idea . . . one that brewed and brewed, but you just let it sit?

Then, one day you see an ad on the internet for YOUR PRODUCT or CONCEPT. Someone else had the same idea and made it happen and you think, *Oh No! That was MY idea!* But you never followed through. Crushing, wasn't it?

In the world, because of Collective Consciousness, similar currents and ideas are running everywhere. Chances are other people are feeling the same pull to your concept or something similar, and will eventually present it. So you should do it! You can be the first, or you can create a better version of a current concept.

No matter how innovative, grand, or ingenious your idea is, if it sits inside your head without you taking action, that's where it stays.

In order to make our dreams come true, we must take action rather than simply wishing for what we want.

Daily Om

When some other maverick or entrepreneur brings your big idea to market you will end up beating yourself up . . . so take action now. In today's world, the idea of combining purpose with a passion to solve a problem or create an opportunity is creating social entrepreneurs everywhere. You could be one of them.

Or are you afraid?

Taking a leap is a big deal and it's easy to come up with excuses or feel someone else could do it better. Believe me, when I was just starting out in the world, it was my oyster. I planned to be the editor of *Vogue* magazine and make a million dollars. Now, many years later, that exact dream has not transpired. BUT, a different path presented itself along similar lines and I was lucky enough to have a second chance to pursue a career of fashion and compassion, passion, and purpose.

It's easy to get stuck in a rut and allow self-doubt and imposter syndrome to creep in. In fact, I would dare to say many people in the world are treading water, not taking risks, afraid to break out, to break away, to make a new start.

Perhaps it's your family, a dead-end job, or a feeling of obligation that daunts you. For me, it was a stagnant partnership and an obligation I thought I had, which truly did not exist.

So how do you take action and make your BIG IDEA a reality?

My BIG idea had been brewing for some time. I had been diligently doing research, collecting ideas, and cataloging resources to create the perfect concept. But somewhere deep down inside, I must have been telling myself it had to be perfect, or it might fail.

Part of my hesitation was due to my current and struggling business partnership.

In 1984 I had started a women's accessory business and brought on a partner to help me take it to the next level. After enjoying years of success, the kismet was waning. We were both finding our attention was flowing in other directions, and things just weren't feeling as aligned as in the early days.

Then that fateful day came when I learned she had started another business on the side with her boyfriend. I was completely blindsided. I knew that things hadn't been feeling quite right, but I hadn't thought it was THAT bad! I felt betrayed and confused. Especially because we had been best friends and partners for all those years, and I had felt an obligation to her, which she clearly didn't feel to me.

We both had been feeling stuck, and something had to move. Have you ever been in a relationship or partnership that was stagnant, yet you stayed too long because it was the easy way out? I loved my partner like a sister and didn't want to hurt her feelings. Luckily for me, she was feeling the same way and made the bold move to move forward for herself. After many tears, and some soul-searching talks, we realized we needed to sell our business and each of us needed to explore new passions and opportunities that would fulfill our individual interests. To be honest, I was a bit scared, but it was one of the catalysts I needed in order to push me forward.

Before my partnership with her (when I had started and was running the business on my own), I had always been very strong-minded. I was a quick decision-maker and a risk-taker.

However, what happens in many partnerships—as it did in mine—is that I lost my autonomy, with all decisions becoming joint decisions. Existing in that atmosphere for our eighteen-year partnership had literally caused me to become unsure of my own abilities, including the ability to "start over." I was drowning in a sea of self-doubt.

What had happened to me? I awakened each day with a feeling of hopelessness.

I love to create things that people appreciate and are touched by. Beautiful, meaningful objects . . . ones that when worn or used bring happiness and joy. My vocation in life was in retail and wholesale women's accessories . . . fun and glamourous but EMPTY. The business I was in with my partner had no purpose, so I started soul searching, researching, and visualizing with all my heart.

Today, I am so grateful for what happened and also happy to report that we have managed to continue to grow our relationship in a positive way.

In fact, what happened was a catalyst that helped me to create the business I now believe I was meant to pursue.

A key factor that helped me open my eyes to new possibilities was a book I read: *The One Minute Millionaire* by Mark Victor Hansen and Robert G. Allen.

The premise of the book as I absorbed it was that we are all given gifts and are put on this world to use them. People who have embraced these gifts and become successful using them have a calling from God to help others. This really resonated with me. I knew I had gifts and I knew, deep down, that I was not using them for the higher good.

Have you ever KNOWN that you were meant for something bigger and a life filled with purpose, but did not know where to start? Many people live their whole lives with great ideas and passions but get stuck in a field of self-doubt.

I knew through my work with women, charities, and jewelry that there was a cohesive thread that could be used to weave all three together. Women have worn jewelry and charms for centuries, whereas charities need innovative vehicles to raise funds, retain donors, and spread awareness.

What gifts did I have that could create a cohesive solution? My deep reflections on what I loved and was good at led to my realization that I could take my gifts in merchandising know-how and utilize that to teach charities how to fundraise and raise awareness with their own customized products.

I noticed the convergence of two trends . . . the return of charms as an important jewelry category and the need for nonprofits to provide meaningful items to the women that supported them. VOILA! I had the background, the contacts, and the inspiration I needed to start a new business. I had dug deep and defined my passion, and Charity Charms was born. In my mind, that is. But still, I continued to let it simmer, hesitant to get my idea out there . . .

If you are feeling angst and having problems pinpointing what your purpose and passion might be, here are some questions to help you define them:

- What do you LOVE to do?
- What makes you feel free?
- What brings you JOY?
- What are your most treasured accomplishments?
- What can you do with your "eyes closed"?

Reflect on these five questions and answer them truthfully . . . just to yourself.

You may be stuck in an engineering job and should actually be a chef, a travel agent, or an actor. So many of us have taken a path in life that neither brings us joy, uses our gifts, nor fuels our passion.

But you can fix that!

Another exercise I did, besides reading *The One Minute Millionaire* and answering the five questions above, was to start collecting brochures, photos, quotes, and so on. Everyone has their own system they are comfortable with (Google Docs, Pinterest, OneNote, physical articles and photos, etc.,), but the idea is to gather collateral to fuel the vision of your idea.

For my vision, I started collecting brochures from organizations I thought would be interesting to work with, and that was the nexus that birthed my idea for Charity Charms. Truly. One day I had poured a fresh glass of iced tea and spread the brochures all over my dining room table.

I looked down and what jumped out at me were the amazing logos and icons that each organization used to brand its mission. Those icons could make beautiful charms!! Charms that women supporting those organizations would love to wear. (Who doesn't like to talk about the passions they are involved with?) Charms for charities could provide a talking point for women involved with causes, schools, and foundations throughout the world.

Finally, all that searching, seeking, and research jelled into the BIG IDEA that defined my passion, and Charity Charms was born.

Now What?

Luckily for me I had a major breakthrough in the form of a gift from a dear friend.

One night I was sitting with Jennifer, drinking a glass of wine and sharing ideas with her about my concept, and the impact it could make.

She got very excited as most people did when I explained my vision for this BIG PASSIONATE IDEA with huge impact for the world.

Then a really big breakthrough happened. My dear friend gave me an unexpected gift three weeks later.

Jennifer had taken the name I decided on—Charity Charms—and had a designer she knew create a logo and mock up a letterhead and a business card. Then she presented it to me as a birthday gift! I was absolutely speechless. It was like my idea had come to life and was a real product and concept. Having someone support me so much was the second catalyst I needed to launch my new company. Her very thoughtful gift was just the lift I needed to help me believe in myself again. It's phenomenal to imagine the impact just one person can have on another's life with a simple thoughtful act of kindness.

Charity Charms had come to life.

My concept for Charity Charms is to take a centuries-old item, CHARMS, and create them in a new way, based on the icon of a logo. Simply a new twist to an existing product category. Further, these charms would provide an upscale item, created from an organization's logo, that women would actually want to wear—instead of the usual keychain, mug, or t-shirt. Organizations would now finally have beautiful sterling silver items to utilize as vehicles to support the causes near and dear to their hearts. Charity Charms could be used to raise funds and awareness for causes throughout the world! Organizations could use them for fundraising, member recognition, donor and volunteer gifts, and as a unique way to engage their community.

I had found a way to combine my two passions: fashion and compassion into a business that would make a difference. What JOY!

The rest is history. Since 2004, Charity Charms has created custom charm programs for over five hundred organizations worldwide with a value of over $20 million in social impact.

Interestingly enough, Nike launched the Lance Armstrong wristbands the very same month that I launched Charity Charms. Two different but similar ideas—jewelry for charity. We were mavericks in what is now an entire industry, a whole new category, called "Cause Jewelry"; it has been embraced by companies worldwide. Tiffany, James Avery, Kendra Scott and more now have special charms and jewelry for charity.

So it CAN be done, but sometimes it takes the right catalyst(s).

I had two big catalysts really . . . my split with my business partner and my friend's beautiful gift.

All I needed was to believe in myself, gather my tools, and make a plan.

Have you ever done something over and over because you were good at it, then realized it could have a much deeper meaning and impact than you ever thought? Something that comes naturally to you . . . like gardening, art, cooking, or helping people in trouble. I believe we are each born with gifts and it's our God-given mission to use these gifts to contribute to the world. But so many of us take these gifts for granted, and don't realize the power in our hands to make significant contributions . . . and live our passions.

Do you have gifts that you take for granted? Are you living an unfulfilled life because you are not using your gifts?

Seven Steps

Here are the seven steps I recommend to get you started:

1. Define what drives you . . . does Your Big Idea align with your values?
2. Visualize your success.
3. Believe in Yourself and Your Gifts.

4. What is in your wheelhouse to make your Big Idea a reality?

5. Make it come to life—name it, draw it, write about it.

6. Surround yourself with believers and mentors.

7. Map it out, using time, effort, resources, finances.

These are the same seven steps I used, and that I now use to lead my clients through strategy sessions for their "next chapter." And for their outreach to their customers and stakeholders, since they are just as important for businesses as they are for individuals.

It might seem hard to believe, but you deserve the best, especially when times are challenging or life just isn't going your way. It's true!

You deserve to take your visions, dreams, and hopes and make them real, to live a miraculous life. Living your dreams and finding your purpose are the most important things you can do to empower yourself and become a greater light in the world.

Sadly, most people will live their entire lives feeling disconnected and disempowered, never uncovering what they were put on earth to do, not knowing who they really are.

Starting a business from your BIG IDEA is not easy, but if you are doing what aligns with your passions and goals it will flow like water downstream.

Change is the only aspect of life that is constant. And to live an inspired and successful life you must be true to yourself and your vision.

YOU need to be happy, YOU need to be fulfilled, YOU deserve to make your BIG IDEA a reality and YOU are the only one who can make it happen.

You need to have a vision and you need to take action. But the most important component of the success equation is to believe. Ask for what you want and start initiating a positive conversation with yourself and the Universe.

Bringing your BIG IDEA to life and birthing your dream will take hard work, action, reflection, and perseverance. It may morph through several versions along the way. When you follow the seven steps above to create your roadmap, you will find the path to fulfill your purpose in life.

Kay McDonald is a social entrepreneur, author, and coach. She enjoys helping others define their dreams and purpose by finding their BIG IDEA. In the world of cause marketing and product marketing, Kay is a maverick. Her years of experience in the retail and wholesale industry were the catalyst to launch her innovative concept, Charity Charms, which specializes in custom logo branded jewelry. The company was launched in 2004 to fulfill the need for quality, meaningful gifts that organizations could use to engage and thank the members of their community. As one of the country's first socially conscious brands, Charity Charms provides significant and visible items that are more sustainable than the usual branded products.

*Kay's newest "Passion Project" is an interview series to highlight the work of her clients, and women making an impact in the world. She has always believed charms are wearable symbols that have the power to tell a story, connect people in meaningful ways, and build a legacy of love. Her interviews culminated in a compilation book and a new line of sterling symbol charms, which can be found at **charitycharms.com**. Kay is passionate about helping other social entrepreneurs launch their ideas and she offers a coaching series to help them succeed. She is the Founder and CEO of Charity Charms and author of* The Power of Charms. *You can reach her at **kay@ charitycharms.com | 800.615.3120**.*

Scenes from a Crime

*Using "Cinematic Memories" to Release Trauma
and Revision Your Life Story*

by Mary Lynn Navarro

Cinematic Clip #1, Late 1970s, "The Awkward Ride"

*Opening wide shot, deep focus: a residential street,
punctuated with wooded patches, bold trees, and modest
homes built post-Second World War. In the left corner
frame, a car enters and moves toward a patch of woods to
the right; the driver's side hides under a weeping willow.
A young woman is seen; her back is in the frame. Her
peasant dress, looking like a Little House on the Prairie
costume, sways with her measured gait.*

*YOUNG WOMAN enters the passenger side under the
tree. Once seated, she brushes aside her long straight hair
from her face, turns, and nods silently to the driver, her
father. He says nothing as he starts the engine, driving
out of the frame, then tracking along a quiet road,
crossing the world's longest suspension bridge, and
driving onto an urban street until he stops—in front*

of the city courthouse. This is where the woman is set to testify in a trial against the man who raped her.

And here is the spoiler: Unbeknownst to her, however, and in defiance of her hard-fought courage, this trial will be stopped dead in its tracks . . . by her father.

··•◆•··

This is one of my cinematic memories based on a real-life incident of experiencing rape when I was nineteen years old. To address my chapter title, however, there was not just one crime here; symbolically, there were many—from the community shaming that people gave me, police exploitation, and even my own subsequent, self-sabotaging life choices. I have had to liberate myself from traumatic memories in order to be free, to live with integrity in each moment. Thus, the purpose of writing this chapter is to share this process so that you, too, might explore your life, using your imagination to heal and free yourself.

Additionally, this process can be used as a powerful practice for healing practitioners. And if you are a writer or visual artist, this technique can unlock your creativity when facing writer's block or creative nonflow due to unresolved trauma.

Before I developed this technique, I experienced trauma in repetitive, intrusive memories playing as "reruns" of old movies in my mind. Whether they appeared as short clips or full features, my life traumas unspooled in episodic drama. And the resulting damage from these traumas—the lack of support and feelings of betrayal—played out in real relationships. The revisioning technique came about when I dug into the details of my memories, instead of fighting them or continuing the senseless arguing in my head or allowing them to overtake my will. I've studied film techniques, and I often used my love of classic movies, noir, and arthouse films to escape or inform the emotions I was experiencing. So, inspired by my favorite filmmakers, I decided to write out my trauma, re-envision it, and revise it in a creative process.

I deliberately use the word "revise" because it is intended to mean both the new vision and the revising process through writing. This process is called "cinematic" memories. I am not doing standard film script; rather, I am using prose and the imagination of cinema as inspiration and form.

The opening of this chapter is one example—a cinematic "clip." It was liberating to take the image and craft a scene that captured the quiet isolation and awkwardness I felt as a young woman facing this hard episode and the subsequent betrayal of trust by my father.

One late summer afternoon, in a quiet beach area, I was raped and left beaten. I had just finished the shift of my summer job at a swim club and was on my way home, which was quite a distance away. While I was waiting for a bus, a young, handsome man stopped his car, chatted me up, and offered me a ride. I decided to take it. After we drove off, he took an abrupt turn and headed to a desolate beach.

I knew I was in trouble. Doors were locked. I couldn't escape. He threatened to kill me, and after he put his hands around my throat, strangling me, I stopped resisting. After the rape, he left me lying on the dirt road. As he drove off, I memorized his license plate number. I hesitated for a day before reporting it to the police out of fear. I had managed to get home, wash and change, and keep it secret from my family. With the support of my best friend at the time, I finally went to the police. They insisted that I tell my father, which felt like a confession of guilt, as though I were to blame for having been raped. The man was apprehended, a trial ensued. But my father had already determined that he would stop it without letting me know. My father ordered me to keep this forever secret from my mother and everyone who knew us, although of course people found out anyway.

We never spoke about it again.

Never once.

Even back then, I tried to write it out in diary form, but I was so afraid my mother might see it—she had a habit of secretly going through my personal things—that I stopped. I picked it up years later, but the energy to continue writing about that violation against me had passed. I had become a tortured soul with chronic depression accompanied by obsessional, ruminating thoughts about all the past injustices I had suffered and the bad choices I continually made. I could not stop the flow of negative thoughts, even though I tried many techniques, went through the requisite therapy, and embarked on various paths throughout my life. Still, I could not gain a handle on how to move on from emotional torment.

The experience of these thoughts as visual intrusions—the movies in my mind—rendered each sensation fresh, no matter how many times I had experienced it before. In my life, trauma has repeated with no resolution, always appearing like nonstop movie reels. This is, of course, how trauma operates.

Until I became cognizant of these movie memories, the reruns of old plots and relitigating of past injustices only deepened the pain.

I lived most of my life in survival mode; basking in the big struggles kept me stuck in them. Manifesting a gratifying, abundant, and purposeful life when I was always on the edge of nail-scraping survival was difficult. But that was not the worst of it. The worst was far deeper—I experienced thoughts of suicide at the moments of despair and suffered unrelenting self-persecution. One day I had an epiphany. After allowing the images to flow without judging them, I realized that I had been traumatized by the way I was treated as a young woman going through this ordeal. I felt alone and unsupported. But even more than the actual attack, I was re-victimized by my father's treatment of me, the shaming secrecy around the incident, followed by the all-male police investigators sexualizing me, as if branding me with a "scarlet letter" of R, making me feel raped yet again, and finally, by the small-mindedness of people—women included—who condemned me for "giving in," casting me as a pariah.

But I know that I was already traumatized before that incident. It did not set me up for failure; failure was already there, although the secret of the rape reinforced the ever-present feeling of self-contempt.

The following cinematic clip is based on my interview with a detective, alone, before I had told my father.

Cinematic Clip #2, "A Girl Gets Grilled"

It is 1977, an urban police station. A GIRL in denim bell-bottoms and a loose t-shirt enters the screen. We see her back; her long straight hair hangs like a curtain. The camera cuts to a wide angle shot from her perspective. A large, dull-beige rectangular room full of men—a police station. The plumes of cigarette and cigar smoke create low-hanging clouds.

As though moving through mist, the GIRL passes each man as the camera zooms to close-ups: one man, in a suit and tie, turns to stare. His eyes roll up and down her body. Another uniformed police officer bent over a desk pauses, straightens, turns to her, and glares. The buzzing of radio calls, the ringing of telephones, and the clamor of loud talk subside while she passes each one's desk.

[If one did not see or notice that the men were in uniform, this could pass for a men's club, or an illicit gambling room.]

GIRL *(arrives at the far end of the room and knocks at the door of a smaller private office.)*

PLAINCLOTHES DETECTIVE *(opens the door)* Ya better be clean, young lady, cawwse the DA will do an awwtopsy on your stawwry.

[Here are some highlights of the questions, minus the New York accent.]

PLAINCLOTHES DETECTIVE. Do you wear a bathing suit on your job? Were you wearing a bathing suit when you got into the car?

Are you a virgin?

How long did the act go on for?

When did he ejaculate?

Can you say what his male organ looked like? Any distinguishing features?

GIRL. It was . . . I'd rather not.

PLAINCLOTHES DETECTIVE. Anything. It helps to confirm your story . . . Evidence.

GIRL. I don't know. *(Long pause.)* Here. *(She hands him a piece of notepaper.)*

PLAINCLOTHES DETECTIVE. What is this?

GIRL. A description . . . um, a metaphor.

PLAINCLOTHES DETECTIVE. A metaphor? *(He chuckles.)* Hey, Joe, come in here. *(He does a sidebar whisper with the police officer called Joe and both men struggle to contain their laughter. The officer takes the paper and exits, still trying to suppress his laughter.)*

GIRL. Can I have my paper back?

PLAINCLOTHES DETECTIVE. No, we have to hold on to your . . . *metaphor. (The paper reads "metaphor" spelled out.)*

··✦✦✦✦✦··

Here, I intended to right the wrongs of my humiliation and take back my power. In the first clip, "The Awkward Ride," I wrote it flat, without satire or humor according to the way it played out in real life, choosing details to emphasize what I wanted to reveal. It feels dead-on true to the actual event. Memories can be faulty, and I want to point out that for the second clip it was more important to deal with the shame than to set the record straight.

In "A Girl Gets Grilled," I transformed a painfully humiliating moment into a bit of satire—this felt freeing. In further revising it, I could animate the young woman, create an avatar, or I might keep it the way it is and embellish it with more satire. My aim is to emphasize the power to transform a moment of exploitation. For example, I see close-ups of their faces—like in a Federico Fellini film—exaggerated, chomping on cigars, eyes widening and then narrowing as they stare. I hear a melody as the young woman, the girl, saunters by. It could be the Brazilian 1966 classic hit, "The Girl from Ipanema." Or if I wanted to play with a current song, it would be something from Cardi B, such as "I Like It."

I would show close-ups of faces leering and salivating, while strengthening the music; another possibility—a carnival tune to add to the circus atmosphere. I would slow-motion her walk, really slow it as they leer, and then go back into a regular pace; then I would end it by moving the image from the sexualized woman to that of a very young woman, a girl, in jeans and a t-shirt, simple and unrecognizable from the image the men see.

It shifts the humiliation from the woman to those men. It also is not mimicking reality, but embellishing it by releasing the memory in a fictional form of writing. In rewriting my memory this way, I feel particularly good about it—I am chuckling to myself as I see it. My cinematic memory is now a satiric comedy to me, even if you, the reader, do not feel it. The point is that I do. This writing is for me first, like a diary, but instead of facts, I'm using imagination. In imagination, I set myself free.

Cinematic Clip #3, "Jail Time"

Mid-1980s in a provincial town, central California.

Close-up of a nest of purple atop a head, the camera pulls out to a wide angle. It is the face of THE WOMAN—the shot widens—interior of a car, passenger mirror, driver in the front seat. She leans in, slides her finger across the edges of her lower lip, the extra bit of red stain. Then she fastens a waist-length black wig over the nest of her hair. She sets several hair pins in place as she lowers her head, straightening out the hair. The camera cuts to a shot of her feet. She slides open sneakers off her feet (no laces), first one, then the other. There is a rustling, then we see her putting on black spike heels. More rustling as she moves about, then we see her head bent over as she rummages through a duffle bag.

A MALE VOICE. Are you ready? *(The camera fades.)*

A wide shot. It is two hours later, around 10 p.m. THE WOMAN is surrounded by police and handcuffed. She is escorted to a police car. Her driver tears off in her car, speeding away from the scene. Angle from the car interior, the back of her head. She is watching him leave from the back window.

Cut to interior of a jailhouse.

THE WOMAN is seated at a table, hands folded. The camera rests on her face: it is still, quiet. Male voices are heard in the background. She is instructed to stand for a photo.

Camera still shot on her face: it is frozen, plain lips are pressed tight like a straight line, tinged with faded cherry stain. Her eyes are swollen, black rimmed.

THE WOMAN *(her pursed lips open slightly, in a tiny voice)* Can I change?

A MALE VOICE. No. You're in a lot of trouble, young lady. *(Voice fades. Camera fades to black.)*

Another camera shot widens to THE WOMAN'S *full body as she stands against a gray wall.*

THE WOMAN *tugs at her black corset, laced at the bodice, lifting it up, primly. Then she rests her arms by her side as if at attention. The camera pans her full costume: fishnet stockings, garter belt, spike heels, and the waist-length black wig. A flash of light fills the screen, the clicking of the camera is heard, one flash, then another. An unseen person is taking her picture.*

A MALE VOICE. Turn around. Bend over.

THE WOMAN. What?

CHIEF. That's not necessary.

A MALE VOICE. Chief, we have to capture her . . .

CHIEF. It's in the report.

THE WOMAN *turns. More lights flash; another picture has been taken. The camera fades.*

THE WOMAN. Can I change now?

A MALE VOICE. Sit down.

Cut to table in the jailhouse. THE WOMAN *is seated at one end. Hands are folded on a desk. Still in costume, the wig is off her head and she rests her hands on it, as if it is a pillow.*

A MALE VOICE. We need to know more. Are you on your own? Just delivering?

Silence. Camera cuts to The Woman's face. Her lips are tight, head looks down to her hands.

A MALE VOICE. If you could just give us a name, we might be able to do something for you.

THE WOMAN. It's show business . . . *(pause)* seriously, I just came here for the half-time show. I'm the half-time showgirl.

A MALE VOICE. Showgirl?

THE WOMAN looks up to see on the opposite wall the shadow of a sheriff's hat, the police chief.

ANOTHER MALE VOICE. Casey's.

ANOTHER MALE VOICE *(pause)* C'mon . . . you were doing a live sex act?

ANOTHER MALE VOICE. Casey has a show now? This????

THE WOMAN. No, no, I wasn't. It's an act.

A MALE VOICE. *(his voice rising, like a scolding teacher)* That's what it looked like to me.

THE WOMAN. You must be kidding.

ANOTHER MALE VOICE. Casey's? *(pause)* The sports bar?

ANOTHER MALE VOICE *(pause)* If you're not willing to help us, then . . . *(Voice fades)*

At another end of the table, we see the hands of a man. His hands open her duffle bag. The camera cuts to her face, plain and stoically observing, then cuts back to the invading hands tearing into her bag, turning it upside down, emptying out all the contents like captured prisoners: one open red lipstick (cover missing), mascara, crumpled balls of dried snotty tissues, hairpins, gray track pants, laceless converse sneakers, a pack of cigarettes, a small mini-bottle of vodka, tampons, a notepad, an AAA roadmap, socks, sweatshirt, a red bra, a book by Krishnamurti (cover torn), an audiocassette of Echo & the Bunnymen, another cassette of Catharina "Nina" Hagen, a piece of a Kitkat candy bar, out of the wrapper and in broken pieces tinged with white edges, a schedule book...

MALE VOICEOVER *(calling out loudly)* One cosmetic item, one liquor bottle about *two* ounces, one pair of shoes, one pack of cigarettes...

THE WOMAN AS VOICEOVER. Can I ask a question?

MALE VOICEOVER. What—the phone call?

THE WOMAN AS VOICEOVER. No. Can you save me one ... Please?

Camera zooms in on male fingers moving from inside the red bra to the cigarette pack, rolling over each cigarette, unraveling each one slowly. Pouring the tobacco on the table and sifting through. She quietly murmurs to herself a lyric from the song "The Killing Moon." Voice sings "Fate | Up against your will." Her fingers unconsciously move to slightly touch the center of her breastbone.

MALE VOICEOVER. No, this has to be done.

VOICEOVER OF A DIFFERENT MALE. What's that thing on her head? *(A shot widens to the shadow of the side angle of a sheriff's hat.)*

THE WOMAN. My hair? *(Camera zooms in on her hands, on the table, resting on top of the black wig. Fingers pick at chipped black nail polish.)*

MALE VOICEOVER. That purple thing.

THE WOMAN. My hair.

The camera zooms in on THE WOMAN's face. She lowers her head slightly, looks at her watch, it's 1 a.m. Her fingers again graze across her breastbone in the crevice where the small packet of snowy powder, methamphetamine, hidden, rests tightly under the corset. She lowers her head.

The camera zooms in on a close-up of the purple bun on her head. It looks like a bird nest.

MALE VOICEOVER. One prior. Keep her . . .

Fade.

··◆◆◆◆··

I originally started to write this clip, also based on an actual incident, as a creative nonfiction story, in which there are far more details and a narrative story structure. I then turned a small segment of it into this bit of script so I could write freely about this profound moment of self-humiliation, just as in an earlier encounter with police, this time actually with sheriffs. In this one, all the men were "male voices"—imposing voices of authority.

In one shot, we only see the male hands touching her bra—which looks violating—and then unraveling the cigarettes to see if there is any illegal substance inside the cigarette. We also see the woman in disconnected screenshots of hands, feet, head, and wig—as if the whole person is cut up into these images. The jarring cuts are my attempt to create a visual portrait of disconnection and fragmentation.

When the woman is standing in the costume, only then do we see her whole body. Seated, with her smeared makeup, chipped nail polish, and tiny voice, she appears defenseless. At the beginning of the shot of the neon-purple bun, the "bird's nest" symbolizes the nest of trouble; it was a 1980s punk-inspired look. (I did have a disastrous purple dye job that burnt my hair.)

Although the outfit would be looked upon as sexy, there is something off about it. Was it just weird and not sexy? I wanted to convey that idea through the lens and the dialogue; for example, when one of the officers says "That??" in reply to her being a half-time showgirl at a typical sports bar on Monday night football.

I was arrested on charges that included lewd and lascivious conduct and soliciting, with an investigation into drug dealing. It was indeed perilous to be in this situation, possessing illegal drugs, under arrest—my second arrest. Men of the law again were acting questionably; taking photos was a breach of protocol and it seemed quite wrong for police to be doing that, even then.

These three clips comprise a "trilogy" that together encompass the themes of shame and patriarchal authority. There is a good deal more going on here, including why I had gotten into this to begin with, but it's a long story.

I had begun an account in the creative nonfiction story by creating a different character. At first, she was a composite of different women I had encountered in Los Angeles who were involved in the fringe sex and entertainment world—strippers, female wrestlers, singing telegram girls, models for magazines like

Hustler, wannabes who never made it in Hollywood. And there were a lot of drugs in all of it.

But then the character took on its own life. It was a way to enable me to explore the dark parts of myself and my life at that moment. The cinematic technique helped me to become unstuck. This incident had been so hard to write because of the humiliation I felt from my own actions. I'd wanted to write about it for so long, but I was stuck from censoring myself. The truth of the incident is far murkier than what I just presented—I would often say to myself, how the eff did I do these things? Was that really me?

I used the cinematic memory technique to probe it from different angles and to create another protagonist, a new character. Coming in at different angles—as if my mind is the camera looking from a totally different perspective—adds insight that otherwise might not be discovered. All of these clips have enabled a feeling of release and freedom, of unpacking, peeling away, removing layers and *samskaras* (Sanskrit for "impressions"), and letting it all out, even though the piece above feels restrained to me.

I have the version of the creative nonfiction to go back to so that I can continue with detail and actually write the whole story. Were I to work on this clip more, however, I might see it as a montage, a moving visual, slightly Cubist. The oddball art student in me wants to "create art" even though it is actually therapy. But if I wanted to go full cinema, I would play with the idea of horror, a vampire or dark creature motif. There is a punk/goth element to it—the costume, the punk rock music, black nails, and wig—the overall look.

One might ask why these are called cinematic memories? And how does this process help transmute trauma? The reason I call these "cinematic memories" instead of something simpler, like mind movies or visions, is because I become the creator rather than remain a passive recipient.

When I experience an intrusive memory, it jolts my senses into an unwanted, full physical sensation, a form of physical and psychic pain, and deep discomfort that intensifies relentlessly. When the memory—which is just like a movie—comes up, the accompanying emotional and physical charges make it feel as if I am still in the traumatic moment, no matter how many years ago it transpired.

In the past, when I was tortured with these intrusive movie memories, there was no end to them or any way to consciously stop them. So I decided to work with them in earnest. My cinematic memories of the time I was raped, and especially the aftermath, came from working with the mind's version of the memory. Many memories are in pieces or dreamlike. This memory, however, burned grooves in my brain. (There is a dearth of scientific and medical evidence of the effects of trauma on the brain.)

Before I take a deeper dive into this practice of transforming trauma, let me illustrate what I think cinema is and how it influenced me in shifting my perspective from that of passive recipient to creator.

The director Alfred Hitchcock is widely known as a "master of suspense." Every plot holds mystery, even the most implausible ones—as most of them are. But if you examine one scene, you will see that there are specific details that do not at first glance seem to be suspenseful. Take, for example, the film *Vertigo*, a critical masterpiece. We do not care that the plot is implausible or ludicrous. We go for the ride to see how it will all end up.

To create the intended effect, Hitchcock precisely crafts each screen shot or *Mise-en-scène*. In the scene where the protagonist Scotty (Jimmy Stewart) first sees Madeleine (Kim Novak), we see her from the point of view of Scotty. The screen fills with Madeleine, supremely elegant, in a gray tailored suit, she is shaped like an hourglass, her platinum hair coiffed in a tight French twist. She is monochrome; even her high arched brows are gray toned. Hitchcock had Novak's hair dyed platinum and rinsed with a lavender hue, so the camera captured the hues, blending the whole image in a dull, silvery afterglow.

Hitchcock crafts a woman who looks like a Greek statue. She is cold, pale, beautiful, and unreal. Think of the poem "Ode on a Grecian Urn" by John Keats. When we later see the duplicitous character of Madeleine as she really is—Judy—her hair color is darker and her makeup is garish and intense, in sharp contrast to Madeleine. Judy wears a cheap, loud, green sweater dress; she looks "low class," earthy, and insecure.

Through each crafted scene, Hitchcock manipulates suspense, not only from the conventional use of plotline, but also by portraying characters through color, shapes, and elements that do not register consciously. Who is this woman? Why has she conned him? She is far from the Greek-statue beauty. The viewer can subjectively relate to a fragmented identity, or to the point of view of Scotty, a person torn over passions who recreates his "perfect woman," only to find her to be a fraud, as if he were in a mirage. This is also the experience of anyone who has dealt with toxic narcissism. And Hitchcock continues to play on the mirage in using Salvador Dali's surrealist imagery within the conventions of plot. (Clearly genius is at work here, but one does not have to be a Hitchcock to do this.)

As viewers, however, we do not examine the details of color and shape or the *Mise-en-scène*; we just feel the effect, and Hitchcock creates great affect—emotional response—in each detail. Now if you are not familiar with old, classic films, here are some current examples of cinematic expression. In the 2017 film, *Get Out,* writer-director Jordan Peele uses a horror motif of switched identity and "body and soul stealing" as a representation of colonization and slavery. The horrors of the real experience are rendered viscerally, shedding light on the lasting effects of the atrocities of slavery and Jim Crow. Viewers can feel this experience, not just know it intellectually.

Another example that most people will recognize is in the movie *Thelma and Louise.* When Thelma exclaims, right before she and Louise face imminent demise, "For the first time in my life I am awake, really awake," we recognize this as her transcendence from her previous numbed and controlled life to one of revelation and freedom. She does not say, "Okay, now Louise, I have transcended because of X, Y, and Z." A recited list would not have had much effect. But in her saying, "I am awake," the viewer experiences a feeling of liberation.

A director I consider to be a cinematic genius is auteur Agnès Varda. In her 1965 film *Le Bonheur,* the screen opens with a full vision of sunflowers and a blaring composition of Mozart's Adagio and Fugue in C Minor. A beautiful young couple share the perfect family life in an idyllic French country village, until the husband takes a mistress. Then he tries to gaslight his wife trying to turn her perspective upside down to justify his own behavior.

The scenery of family picnics in pristine woods, sunshine, and the ever-present sunflowers remains constant as the underlying motif, but it becomes truly horrific for the wife. This juxtaposition of their idyllic and "perfect" family life and its disruption creates a tension that the viewer must resolve. It is not clear, but the young wife appears to take her life, while the husband replaces her with his mistress, as if nothing happened. Varda's imagery, and especially the allusion to Van Gogh's haunting sunflowers, capture both beauty and terror.

These are all examples of how working with imagery, colors, sensations from known works of art or from scenes of nature can open up one's creativity. It's important to keep in mind, though, that there's an enormous difference between relitigating past injustices or foibles—which only serves to keep trauma alive—and revisioning those traumas for the purpose of transcending them.

Even though we know a great deal about trauma, it was worthwhile for me to revisit Judith Herman's seminal 1992 book, *Trauma and Recovery*, one of the first texts that introduced me to trauma studies. Trauma may stem from an actual incident, a crime against humanity, a personal injury, and so on. Depression and other mental, psychological, and physical struggles usually come with trauma.

Reading Herman's clinical study gave me the "permission" to see my trauma and not deny it. Today, there is a better understanding of trauma and a multitude of modalities and treatments. I would never claim that writing techniques could take the place of medical treatment or therapy. That said, many of us have done a lot of work. After being in different types of therapies and utilizing numerous practices, I now have a willingness and readiness to release what is left.

For me, what feels unique about trauma as compared to other challenges is its repetition. My experience of repeated trauma is that it is an energy that needs to be moved. And its recurrence in real life is the manifestation of what is unresolved. I selected what was constantly recurring in my thoughts, saw the patterns to my story, and recognized how life then played them out accordingly.

What I have discovered in this is that there is a truth I need to uncover, a "golden nugget" of truth from each incident. Locating this nugget of truth led to my breakthrough. And I will elaborate on that further after presenting more about what this entails.

My nugget of truth was recognizing that I have carried shame for most of my life, not just from what happened but also by my own actions in response to it. I kept that shame alive and proliferated it unintentionally. What I want to accomplish now is not just feeling resolved about the trauma, but to change my own behavior around it by not letting trauma rule over my thoughts and actions in life.

Doing this either as a basic exercise or as experimental writing gives way to stories that have been suppressed by the ever-present underlying shame that trauma brings.

So, what is tugging at you to get your story out? Dive into it.

···◆◆◆◆◆···

Here are examples from friends I have worked with on their writing: First, the cinematic clip:

Cinematic Clip #4, "The Honeymoon"

> *The scene opens with nineteen-year-old HERMAN and eighteen-year-old SONJA lying on a thin patch of grass together, in each other's arms, partially hidden under a large tree, where brown, gold, and ochre leaves have*

begun to fall. It is pastoral, a landscape of forest and meadows; a sheep drifts by in the back corner of the screen.

HERMAN wisps a leaf over SONJA's face, stopping at her lips. He kisses her. They are newlyweds. Then, the camera shot widens. At first, the foreground is out of focus. But then the screen shot focuses sharply on a bare wooden shack, a barrack. In front, a disheveled and forlorn group of shabby, worn-down people assemble in a line and, with the tip of the bayonet held by an SS guard, they are marched out of the camp in unison, to meet a cattle car, stationed by the railroad. The next shot cuts to HERMAN whispering to SONJA, "Don't worry, they all like me. We are safe. This will all end soon anyway. The Americans will step in and save us." The screen fades to black.

It reopens on a bunk where HERMAN sleeps. Roused by the end of a bayonet, HERMAN gets up and is marched out, led along with a group lined up and sent off to a cattle car.

··✦ ✦✦ ✦✦··

The backstory here is that my close friend from Holland was writing her mother's memoir of narrowly surviving the Holocaust. Her mother, Sonja, sent to Theresienstadt and then Auschwitz, lost family members one by one, including her nineteen-year-old half-German husband who had futilely collaborated with the Nazis to save himself and Sonja.

My friend, who was also plagued with her lack of reconciliation, finally wrote her mother's memoir when her mother was at a late stage in life; I worked with her on a cinematic clip. It combines her written story with this interpretation of real life: Herman, who was in charge of "resettling" Jewish families in Amsterdam, had already turned over lists of Jews before he and Sonja were taken to their first stop, a labor camp. The SS officer in charge liked him: "Are you sure you aren't full German?" Herman knew that his Jewish mother got pregnant from a tryst with a German soldier, Herman's biological father, whom he never met.

What my friend gleaned from this clip was that her mother and Herman—he, an unwitting collaborator—were young and in love, and could not know the scope of what would happen to them or others, or what his actions meant in turning over Jewish families. When Sonja was in the labor camp with Herman, the first stop before being taken to the concentration camps, they had special privileges.

But as soon as it was Herman's time to be sent off to be killed, the naive belief of an eighteen-year-old, coupled with not being able to process what was unfolding around her, gave Sonja a moment of false hope that turned into utter despair.

Growing up, my friend had to process what her mother endured. And her father—a man Sonja married in an arranged relationship after the war—forbade any of them to discuss it. In fact, as a family, they pretended to be Protestant, not Jewish, as per her father's orders. Sonja survived only because the war ended before she was killed or died from illness, and because Herman was able to delay her inevitable fate. Yet Herman could not save himself when a Nazi officer decided Herman had too many privileges and had to go.

My friend worked though her own trauma by writing and creating her memoir and scenes. In writing this cinematic memory clip, we first see a pastoral scene of young lovers. The viewer is then surprised when the shot opens to see the young lovers are living in a labor camp. The clip lets the viewer see their naivete—that even amid the Holocaust, young love is trying to thrive, like a blade of grass growing through a crack in the pavement. The clip also allows us to humanize the experience, and raises the question of what a collaborator is or does. My friend published her mother's memoir as a hybrid of prose and graphic images, and this scene is in her book.

Cinematic Clip #5, "Marrying a Stranger"

Another close friend, with a similar story, recounts the effect of the Armenian genocide upon his family. His grandmother was found naked and barely breathing in a vast desert area, having been mass-raped and left for dead. At a refugee camp where she was taken, a pastor gathered the survivors, arbitrarily paired them up with partners, and performed a mass wedding. And this was how his grandmother met and married his grandfather—a romantic story, he would sardonically say.

In the beginning of writing a cinematic memory, we focused on her alone in a desert and found naked, on the edge of death, then finally rescued, only to be taken into a camp and forced into a mass marriage ceremony among barely living survivors—and her new husband, a stranger.

Oddly enough, not long ago my friend's own mother tried to persuade him to go through an arranged marriage. His mother, the product of this brutally forced marriage, insisted that this was "the order of life." The trauma continues. He is writing through this, image by image. This writing has helped him to clarify all the traumatic emotions he has inherited.

Create Your Own Cinematic Memories

Here is a five-step guide to creating your own cinematic memories:

1. **Cloud-bursting ideas:** Use freewriting and drawing, incorporating graphics, a vision board, and anything else that helps your creative flow.

2. **Drafting:** Get down the basics that you want to work with, not worrying about the accuracy or the precision.

3. **Golden nugget of truth:** Locate what is blocked and release it.

4. **Revision of the cinematic clip:** Let the form be the medium.

5. **Resolution:** Enjoy feeling liberated and producing a creative work.

Now here is a tip on locating your "golden nugget" of truth. Sometimes it will become apparent as you continue digging in and writing. For example, after I wrote the clip "The Awkward Ride," I saw that this young woman was truly going it alone, courageously. I never saw myself that way or embodied that feeling of courage until I wrote this clip, in itself a mini-story. Then I saw my young self from a whole different light.

The "Jail Time" clip illustrates a low point in my life in which I was responsible for the bad outcomes I experienced. I couldn't figure out how trauma had led me to such a dark place and I felt that life kept happening *to* me. I couldn't see the entire projection of shame in all these episodes.

When I used my imagination to create another character, that process allowed me to explore feelings and thoughts I had suppressed. I call this tool "me / not me." It allows me to use the memory of what happened to the "me" character, and then invent another character who is not like me at all, the "not me," to create a separation. In coming up with a persona that was not me, it let me create a story in which I could go into the feelings and sensations I wanted to explore, but without stirring up the shame associated with the original incident. You could say that fiction authors do this all the time. But in my way of doing this, I start with a version that I am writing or just recollecting, and then move to a version where it is now not me, but another character, and to a fiction that allows me to go where my mind was not previously willing to go, or was unintentionally blocking my flow, suppressing my breakthrough.

I am using the powers of imagination. The new character lets me go to those more fearful places. The "me / not me" technique is valuable in getting to the golden nugget. And to take it further, it is akin to triangulating the two versions into a new one. When I delved into the fiction of the character, I saw things in myself I just had not acknowledged. I rightly blamed myself for getting arrested and nearly doing serious jail time, but the guilt and shame stayed within me for years. I was reckless, using drugs to self-medicate, embarking on highly risky behavior, throwing myself fully into danger, like a death wish.

When I was about forty and had a breakdown from depression, a psychiatrist gave me a copy of *Trauma and Recovery* by Judith Herman, MD, as I said before. That was when I understood how high-risk behavior is tied into trauma. I began my therapeutic journey. But now, my soul journey has come full circle. I feel freed from it. Applying this technique enabled me to understand other aspects of a disorder. It has led me to a compassionate understanding of my failures and a knowledge of how to release the pain when I tap into my creatorship.

If you are reading this chapter, most likely you are already committed to transformation. I recommend this technique of cinematic memories to add to your toolbox. Furthermore, when working on the golden nugget and the breakthrough, adding in other modalities will help in resolution. Techniques I've found useful are those that allow you to feel what is in your body, including practices of yoga, bodywork, and breathwork.

When embarking on writing, most people think about action and drama, but I recommend also writing in details that are not action focused. Shapes, colors, sensations (even smells) and textures are what get to the truth of what you feel. The drone of "this happened, then this, then that . . . " does not lead to the deeper sense of what you're feeling.

When I rewrite my memories, it is as if my soul is painting the story. I include different examples from directors because it shows the many creative ways you can approach this process. If you are an artist or writer, then you can use this process as a way of producing art that taps into your emotions, empowering your creatorship.

I have found that this technique helps me move the stuck energy of trauma and gain closure. Proof of this is in how I react when I find I am reactivating old trauma—I see it at once. For example, if I'm forming an unhealthy relationship with someone, or I'm in a relationship with someone who themselves is not in a healthy place, or I'm self-sabotaging my career path by not showing up or hiding—I catch this sooner and act. The familiar behavior from past trauma is now transforming, and I act more in favor of my higher good.

Unreliable Narrators and the Kicker to My Story

It might be of interest to address the rationale for my father's actions. At the time of the trauma, I saw his silence and stopping the trial as not standing up for me. I wondered how these behaviors could be justified in a man who did everything to protect his family. My father, proud and dignified, did all he could to provide us with a wonderful life. We had far more material comforts growing up than our neighbors. He fostered education and service to the community. He was responsible for building a community center and dealt with all the complexities of funding it. He also constructed a veterans memorial and he endlessly helped our neighbors, as he was able to build, construct, design, and even do complicated electrical work.

But one thing he had difficulty with was expressing emotions of love. A Second World War veteran himself, my father fought in Okinawa when he was still very young. He grew up with a mother who treated him as a brother, a grandmother who acted as a mother, and a scoundrel father. Over time, I came to understand why he stopped the trial.

Some years ago, decades after this ordeal, I happened to have a conversation with a close family friend who was using alcohol to get out of his recovery. In one of those strange moments you never expect, out of nowhere he dropped a bomb. He started the discussion with, "You never knew what your father did at that time . . . " He then told me a bizarre story filled with revenge and acute violence.

Allegedly, my father, along with a trusted friend who worked in the FBI, went after the man who had raped me. Ganging up on him one night, they flashed knives, tortured him, then beat him just short of death. Then the FBI contact got the assailant fired from his job and rendered him unemployable. His wife had already left him.

The latter part of the story about the FBI contact I find incredible. However, it is not impossible, as I do recall this "friend" often pushed the boundaries of the law. However, I never experienced my father as being a vengeful vigilante. But does this matter to me? No. I am not sure if I even believe it. The story came from an unreliable narrator. But then I thought, *What if it were true? What if I am unreliable too? Are my thoughts delusional?*

When you have had trauma, you will always be prone to self-doubt and re-examination. But all stories in the end are just that—stories. Emotions are real, but emotions have waves and are not the truth of who you are. My advice is that you must get to your own truth. Tune in and listen. In doing this technique and sharing it, I am validating my journey. I am able to see new angles. And next, I might write from the point of view of one of my antagonists. That will be interesting.

As for my father, I recall seeing a picture taken of him when he was around seven. That would be the early 1930s. He is dressed in those knickers that boys wore then; he dons a formal jacket and bow tie, and his hair is side-parted and slicked down. In his Sunday best, he poses with a broad smile. This was the day that his absent father was supposed to visit, take him to get ice cream, and spend time with him. My father waited all day. His father never showed up.

This story is not a cinematic memory I will write because it is not my story anymore. Whatever story that picture tells, the memory remains my father's. I do not see the vigilante—but the little boy waiting for his dad. I am brimming with love and grateful to have had him as my father.

A final thought.

Working with cinematic memories is not just a craft or skill, it is a habit of mind. I do this every day, and now I use my mind to create—I do not have to write everything down when my purpose is to rewrite a distressing moment of my day. I can use my imagination to better serve my higher self, to reinterpret a moment. Moreover, like many disorders, obsessional thought is a lifetime challenge and, even when I feel great, I can lapse into negative thinking for the smallest things. I now have a way that transforms and liberates negative self-talk. Sharing stores helps not only you but others too. Stories heal. We share stories through film, literature, history, art, mythology, folk tales, and lore. Why not share your story by getting it out?

I now feel freer to write full blast on projects that previously left me stifled. A documentary film and creative nonfiction are in the works. I use my technique for parts of the writing and I determine how I want to do this, at what level of work and detail—and you can too. You can write your whole story, or transmute your trauma to a practice of joy and gratitude. You decide. You create!

MaryLynn Navarro, PhD, is an associate professor of English at Kingsborough Community College, the City University of New York, where she teaches writing and research, short story, film, and journalism courses. She has written for academic journals and presented on film, literature and social issues, and has taught for over thirty-five years. Additionally, she currently offers a non-academic, specialty writing course that combines "left brain" and "right brain" activities, somatic writing, cinematic memories with transformational healing modalities. Available for private consultations, presentations on writing techniques, and course information, you may contact MaryLynn at **MLNavarro1@gmail.com.**

Radical Awakening to Your True Self

by Catherine Allan

A re we going to be captured again? I wondered in the early morning quiet. Or will we make it across the border this time?

Huddled under a cold burlap blanket in the back of a covered wagon, my brother, parents, and I felt each other's fear, the only sound our breathing and the soft padding of horses' hooves through the snow. Endlessly waiting and chilled to the bone on this wintry morning, we knew our fate hung by a thread. The farmer kept the horses moving, with our hired guide seated beside him on the wagon, courageously heading toward the border between Hungary and Austria.

Freedom awaited us in a new country. *Will we make it across this time?*

Two weeks earlier, when the Hungarian Revolution of 1956 broke out, our small family of four had attempted to escape. After walking in the snow for hours, close to the border, Hungarian soldiers suddenly came upon us.

"Stop!" one of them yelled.

We were caught. The soldiers asked for our identification papers and then forcefully took us to a concealed campground, where we found many others standing in line. The authorities identified us as traitors to communism and recorded our names. For hours, we stood in line with others who were also trying to leave the country. When we reached the front of the line, the soldiers threatened my father harshly with incarceration if we tried to escape again.

I fainted from the merciless stress and fear of all that had transpired. Would we ever be free again? At night, we lay next to one other, still dressed in our clothing, and eventually fell asleep on the ground inside a huge tent.

The next day, they let us go, telling us to "return home and never try escaping again."

Nonetheless, only a couple of weeks later, my parents' friend Douglas came from the US to Austria and hired a guide in Vienna to take us out of Hungary. When the guide turned up at our door, my dad made arrangements for us to leave the country. Within twenty-four hours, my family and I rode the train again to the end of the line, twenty miles from the Austrian border.

But this time, instead of walking toward the border, our guide took us to a nearby farmhouse. We arrived at 5 a.m. and quickly bundled into the back of a wagon. Freedom and safety beckoned to us a brief ride away in Austria.

By some quirk of destiny, we escaped across the border successfully.

Douglas was waiting for us at a hotel in Vienna with newly bought clothes, knowing that we had escaped with very little baggage. In the middle of the day, without a word, I lay down on the bed in my brand-new sheepskin coat and slept for a long time. My last thought was, "We are safe for now, but where is life taking us?"

Over the coming months, we prepared for a new life ahead. We could never go back now. We learned that life can change swiftly and unexpectedly. Freedom is a precious gift, attainable only for the very fortunate. Earlier, when the Russians rolled into Hungary in their tanks, my parents weren't staying around. They had barely escaped death in the Second World War and had lost faith in communism. There was as much poor health, poverty, addiction, and alienation as before. They discovered that communism was hierarchical, not egalitarian, lacking justice and equality, with greed and control predominating among those in power.

People did not feel free in Hungary, where their education, training, their jobs and homes were chosen for—or rather dictated to—them. Can you imagine all of those aspects of your life not being your choice? If you had an extra room in your house, the government could put a stranger in it—and they did. We had to leave. But now, what would happen to us?

In Austria, within a few days after our dramatic escape from oppression, my parents found distant relatives to stay with until we had enough money to get safe passage to North America on a ship. We were headed to Philadelphia, where Douglas lived, but we learned the US had closed its borders to refugees from Hungary.

Nine months later, sponsored by my uncle, we landed in Montreal, Quebec, Canada. My uncle had escaped and landed there the previous year. Destiny safely brought us to my father's family, and now we had to survive.

The life of an immigrant is arduous, a journey with no easy routes for learning a new language, finding a new job, and earning enough to live on. So my parents placed my brother and me in a disadvantaged children's home—actually, it was an orphanage!

They felt this was essential so that they could work twelve hours a day, six days a week, serving in the hospitality industry as busboy and waitress, in order to earn enough to support us. Within a year, my parents had saved enough to afford a small apartment, and my brother and I could finally go home.

In the meantime at the children's home, my brother and I had to learn not only to speak English but also how to live with strangers whose way of life was very different from ours. We had to adapt to our new environment or suffer hardships of fear, loneliness, and alienation. Quite innocently, I realized early on that, if I remained optimistic about eventually returning to my parents' care, I would feel better, even though there was a lot to overcome before we could be reunited.

I had to *accept my situation, maintain a positive attitude* with those around me, and *appreciate all that I was learning, receiving, and experiencing* in my unfamiliar environment. *Staying calm* within strange circumstances and *having a sense of humor helped* me overlook the faces of children who ignored me, found me strange, and rejected me. *Accepting this uncomfortable situation* helped me endure the strange food and overcome the challenges of not being able to express myself in English.

At the young age of seven, I learned how challenging life can be, whether it was leaving my country under duress, enduring separation from my parents, adjusting to an environment in which people viewed me as odd, or being unable to communicate. It was difficult being without my parents at the orphanage, especially when children picked on me because I was different. However, I noticed that *when I smiled, looked happy, and appreciated others*, both adults and children treated me fairly. At dinner, even though I didn't like turnips, I ate them all and was able to have dessert too!

And when I went to bed at night, instead of disturbing others with my crying when I felt sad, I made myself *think of what I was grateful for that day.* The list was not long, but it did include having my bed close to the bathroom and being able to see the sunshine in the dormitory in the morning. I enjoyed reciting our daily prayers, singing hymns at the table, and eating the desserts.

I discovered that *joy came from facing and allowing what is,* and my happiness grew as I accepted these unwanted circumstances. I learned that *without acceptance there is only struggle. With acceptance, there is the beginning of personal transformation, freedom, peace within, and healthy relationships.*

A year after we arrived in Montreal, my brother and I went to live with my parents again and I started third grade. It took me a few years until I spoke English fluently and felt at home in this new city. I was fortunate enough to find school relatively easy, because I enjoyed learning. Later on, after high school, I went to McGill University, and took a BSc in genetics and biochemistry with a view toward attaining entrance into medical school. However, when I realized I was more interested in counseling people, I took an MEd in applied psychology instead.

Interestingly, in my last year at McGill, through a friend, I met an American who became my husband; we fell deeply in love. We moved to Toronto so that he could establish himself in a career where he didn't have to be bilingual and speak French. Two children and a master's degree later, and now a psychotherapist, I separated from my husband. It became clear that, with all that was going on, we were hardly together as a family and were quickly growing apart because our values differed. No matter how hard we tried, we really didn't have enough in common.

The next ten years was a profound journey of great hardship for me, as a single parent bringing up two boys and working for a child welfare agency. My sons were talented in sports, with good marks in school, and they had friends. They rarely saw their dad and missed him terribly. He seemed busy making a life for himself and seldom took the time to see them. I married again briefly when the boys were in their mid-teens, but again unsuccessfully.

Fast forward a few years, I was still living in Toronto after both of my sons had left home. My older son graduated from University of Western Ontario as a financial analyst and my younger son completed at Canisius College in Buffalo with a physical education degree. Both had begun their careers and were living on their own. I had attained "my freedom" but was not feeling it.

Rather, I was a lonely empty nester still seeking happiness. Aged fifty, I felt life was passing me by. Two unsuccessful marriages left me living alone and still craving for a happy family life. What I didn't realize was that I did not love myself enough and as a result kept looking outside for love and joy.

I lacked a good role model for family life and love. The love in my family of origin was based on putting food on the table and working hard, with little time for family members and self-love. Neither of my parents took the time to look after their own needs. Neither were happy people. I knew I wanted a better life now that both my sons were looking after themselves and I had far less responsibility. I still hoped that perhaps, somehow, I could offer my sons a way of loving themselves, by modeling a happier life.

I had been meditating for a while and was now curious about what it meant "to be fully enlightened." That was the oft-stated goal of meditation, but how would I attain this exalted state? Perhaps that was the answer to my lack of inner happiness. Maybe then I wouldn't need anyone, but could just enjoy relationships without expectations, *love myself, and share that love with others.*

One evening, I was reading an article in the *Earth Star Magazine* that a friend had shared. The article piqued my curiosity. It claimed that I could "wake up from the dream of false identification" in a weekend. The seminar, given by Yukio Ramana, had as its premise—and promise—that "with Radical Awakening" to "Pure Awareness" I would live thereafter in the "ever-present" moment. That sounded like enlightenment to me, and I felt irresistibly drawn to its promise.

But the seminar was in Los Angeles in August and I was in Toronto working with the Ministry of Health. Could I get the time off to go?

To make a long story short, I left for LA a few days before the seminar. On the flight to the retreat, I remember thinking, *I will likely never be the same again.* That proved to be predictive.

The retreat was a weeklong opportunity to receive the Radical Awakening process with about twenty other people at a beautiful setting in the country outside LA. On the morning of my awakening, I entered a room in a lovely country home where Yukio Ramana sat with a smile on his face. A couple of hours and a heartfelt conversation later, while in a meditative state and through our dialogue, I received a transmission from Ramana. *I felt more awake than I had ever been before.* After our session, I walked out into the light of day and felt as though I was walking on air. Everything around me appeared very clear and alive, *my eyesight acute, my feelings and senses heightened. I felt more aware of my surroundings and more present than ever before.* That night, and for the rest of the week, we retreatants meditated during our sadhana gathering. Before leaving, we were asked to share our transmission with many others in our lives.

When I returned home, my life changed entirely. I had been working for eight years with the Ministry of Health as a program consultant, now responsible for over forty-five addiction-treatment agencies' budgets, staffing, and programs. I had traveled all over the province, held endless meetings, and experienced continuous stress without much personal or leisure time. Though I loved the work, it had grown more and more tiring.

All that came to an end after my awakening. I let it all go and began working from my home office as a spiritual psychotherapist, *raising the awareness of my clients through the transmission* that I had received in Los Angeles and would now pass on to others. Since I had already earned my applied psychology degree and was a psychotherapist, I could now work in private practice, instead of as a consultant. It was a natural transition to return to psychotherapy, now with a spiritual focus, one that *soothed my soul*. I felt really empowered to share my newly awakened state.

Awakening is an opportunity to self-realize and begin the work of loving yourself and others. Emotionally, I truly feel the difference. Not only have I learned to release emotional blocks, old beliefs, habits, and patterns causing pain and suffering, but I have learned there are reliable tools that can help anyone focus on keeping their mind in the present moment.

I hear from my clients how they are manifesting their desires and realizing their highest potential more than they ever imagined. They are noticing how *living life with more awareness is truly reinforcing and enriching.* They talk about *being more peaceful and living a life of freedom, service, and joyful fulfillment.*

The questions that have arisen as natural by-products of this work are these: How could Radical Awakening prepare us for a new way of life that is coming out of the worldwide COVID-19 crisis? Since awakening offers a greater awareness to an individual, can it be passed on to enough people to heal our world and create world peace?

With awareness, you begin to realize you are here to serve and to improve the way things have been. You are the *wayshower*. It is up to you to demonstrate your willingness to be more loving, caring, kind, and compassionate. *This brings untold benefits not only in how you feel, but also in your relationships.*

Through the process of Radical Awakening, each of us can share our joy when we feel well and happy, rather than express our unhappiness when we're fearful, angry, or sad. Being more aware, you may still feel a range of emotions, including everything from anger, fear, worry, and suffering, to caring, joy, appreciation, and compassion. The difference is that you are more capable of controlling the very emotions that you want to release.

It becomes possible to demonstrate to those around you that *through managing your feelings, negative emotions no longer hook you for long* and are quickly replaced by trust in your inner guidance and the wisdom that comes from accepting and allowing life to just be.

I had an epiphany the other day! I was alone at the cottage, a place I dearly love and cherish. But I wasn't feeling happy and didn't have any reason not to be. I had woken up suddenly that morning from a dream where I was having a wonderful time in a large group gathering but had left my baby alone. I felt cut off from her, separated, and couldn't reconnect. As I awoke from the dream, I was left with these uncomfortable feelings of separation and disconnection. What could I do? I spent my day in solitude walking in Nature.

The following morning, I woke up feeling better. I didn't know what had changed. But *I felt connected.* I pondered these feelings as I walked along the river and this is what came to me: As I had walked in Nature the previous day, I felt a part of all that was around me and it reminded me of *being fully connected to my Source.* Just as I had been before I was born.

At birth, so many years ago, I physically separated from pure consciousness. Not until I awakened fifty years later did I realize that, in fact, I am still connected to my True Essence that some call God. And I always will be.

You and your family, your community, and every person in communities around the world are the same in that respect. Each one of is truly connected and an essential aspect of our Source.

Realizing that each one of us is an essential part of our Source can help us feel free and powerful. When we awaken to our wholeness, we realize that we are one with everyone and everything. So many saints tell us pure awareness or enlightenment is not selective or exclusive. It has always been this way.

The process of remembering who we truly are may be simple or complicated. It isn't essential that we self-realize in this lifetime or in the next. Self-actualization with the support of our Creator happens *when the time is right for us as individuals.*

What is essential to know is that *you create your own reality.* You can receive all the love, joy, peace, and power to live your dreams. You have the courage to let go of all that no longer serves you and create your life anew. You need not suffer, nor endure the life that appears to be unraveling before you. *You are truly blessed with happiness found within you.*

Okay, I can hear you thinking, *That all sounds really good, but HOW do you do that?* Let me give you some examples.

What makes you smile? For most people, it's someone in their family or a friend, a pet, or some funny experience. Think about it. Do you remember those precious moments when someone cheered you up and how good it felt? Smiling creates *those happy chemicals in you*.

What do you love doing? Whether it's a job or a hobby, each of us loves doing something that makes us feel good. A lot of what makes you feel happy is already present in your environment, and it's often free. Breathing practices and meditation are wonderful ways to enliven the body and calm your mind. Most of us take our *breathing* for granted, but it truly can be even more enriching with daily breathwork practices. *Meditation* can be as simple and easy as sitting still. Yes, thoughts will come and thoughts will go if you let them and just be. There are many free videos on YouTube for breathwork, meditation, and yoga if you're interested.

Here are some options to put your awakened state into practice in your own life.

1. Notice when you are in the present moment (e.g., feeling alive and grounded) and when you are more entangled in your thoughts (e.g., feeling out of touch with your feelings and surroundings, perhaps sad, angry, afraid). Notice the difference. When you become aware of not being present, you can refocus on the moment by letting your thoughts go like clouds in the sky.

2. Use your breathing to slow down your thinking, help you focus on the present moment, calm your body, and feel

more peaceful. Long, deep breathing or a powerful, faster breathing practice can calm your mind.

3. To slow down your racing thoughts, try any form of movement or exercise that you like. Walking, cycling, yoga, swimming, or jogging are some possibilities. Movement gives you a greater feeling of connectedness within.

4. Any creative endeavor calms your mind and helps you focus. This might include drawing, singing, writing, painting, playing piano, knitting, or quilting.

5. Meditation is so much easier after doing any of the other activities mentioned. Meditation is key in bringing you to a restful, peaceful, and awakened state.

The higher your vibration, the happier you are, and the more you are able to share your love, joy, and good nature with others. You and I are here to make a contribution, and each one of us has a role to play in being in this world but not necessarily of it. What is your contribution to your family or community? It can be as simple as a smile, staying positive and optimistic when you're having a bad day, or being compassionate and kind to those who least expect it.

All of these positive feelings add up! They become good vibes, just as random acts of kindness make the giver and receiver feel better. Have you experienced that? I witnessed someone just smiling at an elderly person walking on the street, and it made me smile, too.

Remember, you are always connected to your Source. How powerful is that! Each one of us has a spark of the Creator, a light within our hearts that is brilliant, ever-present, healing, peaceful, joyful, and fulfilling. And just imagine, you can let go of feeling lonely and feel the love of your Creator any time you want. Just place your left hand on your heart and the right hand on top. Breathe deeply in and out, long and deep. After a few minutes of breathing deeply with your eyes closed and sitting comfortably, you will start to feel warmth in your heart area. Just keep feeling the warmth and breathing deeply.

Think about someone you really care about and you'll be feeling even more warmth, and perhaps love, caring, or appreciation in your heart. If you stay with the experience for a bit longer, your vibration will increase and you'll feel so much better for the rest of the day!

You may have noticed the many ways that my life has improved since the beginning of the story about my escape from Hungary. Here are some tools I have used to help me feel lighter and happier.

1. **Being Positive, Staying Calm, and Having a Sense of Humor.** To feel better, I had to maintain a positive attitude with those around me, and appreciate all that I was learning, receiving, and experiencing in my unfamiliar environment. Staying calm within strange circumstances and having a sense of humor also helped.

2. **Appreciation.** Each day, I thought of what I was grateful for. The list was not long, but it did include having my bed close to the bathroom and being able to see the sunshine in the dormitory in the morning. I enjoyed our daily prayers, singing hymns at the table, and the desserts.

3. **Accepting and Allowing.** I discovered that joy came from facing and allowing what is, and my happiness grew as I accepted my unwanted circumstances. I learned that

with resistance there is only struggle. With acceptance begins personal transformation, freedom, peace, and healthy relationships.

4. **Letting Go of Expectations.** Expectations can often lead to disappointment. I feel good when I enjoy relationships without expectations, love myself, and share that love with others.

5. **Staying Present.** So much pain is caused by our negative thoughts and emotions. I not only learned to release emotional blocks, old beliefs, habits, and patterns causing fear, pain and suffering but also learned there are reliable tools as mentioned above that can help anyone stay in the moment.

6. **Being Connected.** Remember, you are always connected to your true self, your Source. Knowing this to be true will make you feel better every time.

And when you are happier, your higher vibrations are felt by others; they rub off on those that need them the most, making them happier. I wish you a good long life—no matter what happens.

Catherine Allon experienced her life changing dramatically when she attended a Radical Awakening session with Yukio Ramana in 1998 in California. She walked out of that session with senses heightened and a still mind connected with Nature and all around her. When people become more consciously aware, they follow their passion and live a life of success, fulfillment, and happiness. Returning to Toronto, she decided to leave consulting at the Ministry of Health and create a private practice bringing greater awareness to people feeling stuck and trapped in their lives.

Since 2000, Catherine has been a spiritual counselor and kundalini yoga teacher, teaching yoga classes with groups and individuals. As a laughter yoga teacher she believes that without humor there is not enough joy, and through service and volunteering we remember to love one another. You may contact Catherine at 416.694.0232; ccawakens@ca.inter.net or energyawakening. com.

Insightful or Insane?

by James Buffalo Moreno

With my heart beating loudly in my chest and my sanity teetering on the delicate edge of reality, I see a glowing orb gleaming in the sky. It's speaking a telepathic dialect that spills from my tongue. The flow of language brings me a sense of inner strength, while I softly whisper these words of beauty into the ear of my friend. I don't know exactly what I'm saying, but I know a force for good and a healing has come to those who are here to listen. The sounds possess great kindness and I feel passionate about being alive. I feel so close to all that is in the Universe. This tributary of tears, rolling on the skin that surrounds my spirit, has a dutiful purpose as it embodies the ocean of gratitude that I'm feeling on this night, a night I will never forget. "Oh, my God. Is this really happening? This can't be happening."

For several weeks, I had been wondering if I was well.

What if I was just making it all up? What if I needed psychiatry and medication?

When I'm sitting at my altar, I feel like the best version of myself. My shamanic practice is my greatest blessing. As I begin my prayers, the smell of sage takes me immediately into the cleansing of the spirit. I can let go and just be. What comes when I'm at my altar overflows with kindness. All that I experience there is a gift.

My mind had been pondering the reason that this work became my path. Of course, I remember clearly when I told a high school teacher that I wanted to be a shaman with the best smart-aleck tone I could muster. I had no idea it was a declaration that the Universe would take seriously. There must have been truth to that statement.

I've often thought, *It would just be easier to be an accountant, or anything else.* In the early days of my practice, my own self-ridicule—not to mention the ridicule of others—forced me to ask the inner question, *What gives me the right to do this work?* My inner voice was saying, *You have to be good beyond others to do this type of work,* and in my life I had experienced all the common flaws of being human. After many hours of prayer and meditation, the answer came to me, *I am good because I am of Creation. I can do this work because it has been given to me. I do it because I can, and for no other motivation. I give time and effort to this practice because it is mine to give.* Listening for the voice of the Creator, hearing the whispers of the inner workings of the life and spirit of others, is just so out of the ordinary.

The things that I see and hear in my mind's eye just flow in. Sometimes I haven't the slightest clue of what I'm saying or why I'm saying it.

One time I told a person, "Under the blue pillow." I apologized because I couldn't give any additional information. I just knew she needed to know "Under the blue pillow." For the most part, I have no idea what happens with the information that I impart to people. In this case, I received a call a couple of weeks later. The person explained that as she was leaving for a job interview and discovered she had misplaced her keys, she had torn the house apart and searched everywhere, including under the cushions of the couch. At the very moment when she said, "If I don't find my keys right now, I'm going to be late! I can't be late!" She caught a glimpse of a blue throw pillow and said out loud, "Under the blue pillow!" She found her keys, made it to the interview on time, and got the job.

Then there was Rose. She was brought in in a wheelchair to a Ceremony at a local center, where I would lay my altar on the ground to pray for those in attendance. She was very sweet and explained that her pain had lasted for about nine years and that she had had to use the wheelchair for that amount of time. I prayed for her as I did for everyone else. I don't remember the words that I gave to her that day, but I remember her gratitude. As she left, I remember thinking what a sweet lady she was, and her adult son was a gentle spirit, too.

She called the center the very next day and asked for my contact information. We spoke by phone briefly, and she insisted that I travel the twenty or so miles to see her. "You have to come today," she said. Upon my arrival there was a woman working in the yard. She was draped in a wide-brimmed hat, shielded from the California Central Valley sun. I got out of my car and the woman stood up. She was wearing gloves and held a small garden spade. She said, "Hello," and I began to ask if Rose was to be found. She took off her gloves and pulled away her hat and sunglasses. It was Rose. Her son came out of the house with a clank of the screen door and a huge smile on his face as he walked down the wooden ramp from the porch.

"Yes!" he said, as I must have had a stunned look on my face.

"This was my joy, working in the yard," she said. "I haven't been able to work in the yard for nine years. My pain is gone."

Her son was just shaking his head at everything she said.

She started to thank me, and I told her, "Yes, I took time to pray, but the healing came from inside you. It's the work of the Creator in you."

Another time I saw the power of prayer unfold was when a loved one came to me and said, "I have been working on my family history and I have gotten far, but I have lost the bloodline."

She said, "I want to continue on, but I can't find any more information." So I prayed at the altar.

After the Ceremony, I said to her, "I could hear the sound of drums, and they were the drums of Africa. There was dancing and celebrating among the women."

Her family was from Mexico, so she was a bit perplexed.

When she continued her search, she found a file marked "Mulatto," an outdated classification for people of mixed European and African descent. Inside the file, she discovered her "Mulatta" (female) ancestor, who opened the way to many more generations.

The story doesn't end there, though. When presenting the family history to the elders of her family, one of them had to face his own depravity. His daughter had married an African American man and he had told the couple that they weren't welcome in his house. Now the detail that they had Mulatto blood in their heritage stared him in the face. The healing was found within him to go to his daughter and her husband and ask for forgiveness. They repaired the relationship and he remained in close contact with them until his passing a few years later.

On the night that the orb appeared in the sky, I was sitting at the altar facing east, as I always do after the cleansing with sage, giving prayers of thanks to the Creator in the directions, thanking the ancestors, Mother Earth, and Water Spirit. I began to pray for my friend. I was picking up pain in her skeleton. I continued to pray.

As I looked up toward the sky, I saw a bright flash that resembled a butterfly or an hourglass, and then it became a ball of light that moved quickly to another part of the sky, unlike any movement I had seen any object make before. Then the telepathic language came.

I needed to put my hand on my friend's shoulder and turn her slightly but quickly. I was kneeling on the ground. I was very close to her ear. I began to repeat what I was hearing. The language had pops and clicks, unlike any language I was familiar with, yet I was talking in a whisper. The orb was changing color and the color changes were giving me changes in my feelings. I felt so much, but I never felt fear. It felt like I was in the presence of an angel. At that point, I didn't know what I was saying, but it felt so good. I knew it was good.

There were two guests present, both sitting still with their eyes closed. I began to repeat a phrase over and over. The orb then departed faster than anything I've ever seen. I turned my friend back toward the altar and resumed my position facing east. I prayed for the others who were present. Then once again, the bright flash appeared in the shape of a butterfly and became an orb. I was guided back toward my friend, and this time I gently turned her east by the shoulders, and the whisper began again, this time in English. I turned my friend back toward the altar and released her shoulders. I sat back at the altar and began to chant the phrase I heard in my mind in the unknown language. It all seemed real and profound.

My personal prayers in the days leading up to this Ceremony had been to allow me to know if I was sick and needed help, or if this work was real. *Was I just making this all up?*

When the Ceremony was over, one of the other participants said, "I kept hearing a name in my head over and over again." She looked at me and asked, "What was it that you kept saying over and over again?"

"I don't know what I was saying, but it was good, very good, the best thing to say."

"You need to find out what you were saying," she said.

Again, I said, "No, I don't, it was just good, I don't need to know."

We all packed up, and I was feeling as though I needed to make an appointment with a psychiatrist to get to the bottom of everything that had happened.

The other two guests left.

My friend said, "First, I've had back pain for a few years, and as soon as you turned me, it went away; it's gone." She then said, "Can I ask you something?"

"Yes. Sure. What?"

"Did you make that light come?" she asked.

"What light?" I said.

"The orb light in the sky?" she said. "Did you bring that here? Did you ask it to come?" She had heard nothing other than the message I whispered in her ear. But we both saw the phenomenon. We saw the same colors in the orb and the same movement; it wasn't in my mind. It was my own answer to prayer.

The next day, I got a call from the Ceremony guest who had insisted that I find out the meaning of what I'd been chanting.

"What I heard in my head over and over last night," she said, "was the phrase 'Ah Kin.' It's what they call a Mayan priest." Once again, she said, "You need to look up that phrase you were saying last night!"

"How did you find out what 'Ah Kin' meant?"

"I Googled it," she said.

"I really don't need to know," I replied, "but I will look up what I was saying, too."

I typed it in phonetically online, with my best guess at the way the Spanish would write it, and hit enter: Axte Incal, Axtuce Mun. An answer came: A Mayan phrase meaning, "To know God is to know all things."

I accept that my path is to recognize the sacred in the ordinary. I accept that everything I do is the ordinary for me.

My brother Bobby recently lost his life due to COVID, despite being vaccinated. We had to face not being by his side while he lay there dying from the Delta variant. When I performed the Ceremony on his behalf, I felt that there was an opportunity for him to recover. I also saw that he had a choice—a choice to stay or to go. My niece Marcina and I saw very similar visions in our mind's eyes as we sat at my altar together praying for him.

My brother released his body the next day.

Recently, I've felt out of place with the interactions in my community over the entire COVID debate. Once again, the lack of clarity in this situation has brought discomfort. The conflict over what to do and how to do it has been very divisive. I have seen families split apart over lack of respect for individual choices. I have seen the closest of friends fall out of sync with each other because they differ in their chosen course of action, when each is simply doing what they think is right for themselves and their family. There was a discomfort in sharing my own personal decisions that led to my course of actions.

During the COVID crisis, I said goodbye to two family members and two friends, all within a short period of time. Hearing the rhetoric while walking through grief was an overwhelming sensation. Wanting mutual respect was simply not enough for me on my spiritual path. I had to take spiritual action.

Many times, I have used a phrase I learned from Janet Attwood: "I want for you, what you want for you." It's a great reminder that there is value in each and every one of our journeys. Allowing others to want what they want for themselves creates a safe place for them to be honest and forthcoming. It helped me to step back and view all of it with a loving perspective. I stayed connected to those I met with extremely different opinions. It alleviated the need for anger, opposition, and "being right."

It is when we find ourselves feeling out of place in the community, in school, with our family, our career, or in our religious upbringing that we are susceptible to fear, which can make us feel like our small, personal contribution is a drop in the ocean of overwhelming circumstances. I encourage out-of-the-box thinking to create innovation and harmony in the world.

There is discomfort in sharing the gifts given to you, whether you are a shaman, an artist, a writer, or an even an accountant. Sharing your gifts has meaning beyond the action in which you knowingly take part. What you give is yours to give. Keeping your skills, talents, or gifts from others due to fear of acceptance does a disservice to you and all who would benefit from the ripple effect of your contribution. Discomfort is a normal part of our continued growth and discovery. When the first creatures made their way out of the primordial muck and onto dry land, they were out of place. Evolution depends on us making our way past our current boundaries in order to ensure growth and survival.

Some of my personal out-of-the-box practices are these:

Using Phrases, Spoken Outwardly or Repeated in the Mind

These are reminders of the connection we share as human beings.

I want for you, what you want for you. This phrase is like a hug. As you speak it, you can't help getting the benefits from it, too.

Come closer. I use this phrase when someone is having difficulty with me, whether it is due to a misunderstanding of my intent or a regrettable decision I've made that has lasting effects on another human being. When recited in my head or spoken outwardly, this phrase allows me to move from the natural reaction to condemn or push that person away in order to avoid the discomfort of an accusation.

This too is for my good. So many times, when something happens that's counter to my expectations and I perceive it as "bad," it turns out to be a blessing or produces the energy for change that opens the door to my highest good. So when an unexpected or unwelcomed event unfolds, I say in my mind, *This too is for my good.* This phrase sets forward the intention and activates the sense to find blessing in any situation.

What phrases do you use?

Creating Awareness Practice in Life

Use these to connect with another in the moment with curiosity and intent.

Imagining the person speaking to you is you. This is something I do when I'm feeling a disconnect from what is being said, or if I'm having trouble following the intent of a conversation. As I listen, I imagine it's "me speaking to myself."

That makes it very difficult to not pay attention. My attention level rises and I'm much more apt to hear the conversation's content. It also helps when I'm not following the intent of the conversation, because it makes me ask the question, "Why would I be saying this to myself?" Oftentimes, I will connect to the underlying emotion or sentiment, or to the simple appreciation of being in the moment.

Seeing the Beauty. I have undertaken a practice of seeing beauty. Being from the West Coast, I had never seen a red cardinal until I moved to the Midwest in late 2016. The first time I saw one, I was struck by the beauty of its red feathers, especially against fresh white snow. Whenever I saw a red cardinal, it inspired me to look at other birds until I saw their feathers with the same energy of beauty. I also have made a practice of this with human beings, artwork, and other things. For example, when walking into a store and seeing a beautiful woman, I make a practice of seeing each and every person with the same energy of beauty.

What out-of-the-box awareness practice do you use?

···✦✦✦···

To this day, I still don't know what my friend and I saw in the sky on that night when I doubted my sanity. I have no explanation for it. I can say that it was validated by sharing it with another person.

I will tell you what I whispered in the ear of my friend, as I was connected to her and everything else in the Universe:

The sky, it knows you and it loves you. The water,
it knows you and it loves you. The wind, it knows

you and it loves you. The trees, they know you and
they love you. The rocks, they know you and they love
you. The birds, they know you and they love you.
The insects, they know you and they love you. The
animals, they know you and they love you. The entire
Earth, it knows you and it loves you. The Universe, it
knows you and it loves you. I know you and I love you,
for all that is, knows you and it loves you.

We cannot let adversity deter us from sharing our gifts, as this sharing is meant to be the catalyst for our growth as well as the growth of others.

James Buffalo Moreno *has been a transformational leader, and a practicing shaman for over thirty years. He is the former Spiritual Leader of Unity of Grand Rapids, in Michigan. James is the author of* The Search for Higher Self: A Whimsical Tale for the Curious Mind, *and* Sunward: Harvest the Life You Want by Healing the Life You Have, *both titles released in the summer of 2022. He is a noted public speaker, workshop leader, business consultant, artist, photographer, and musician. He has worked with thousands of people in the United States and Europe, and has shared his spiritual workshops since 2002. Connect with James at* **jamesbuffalomoreno.com.**

There have been only a few times in my life when I've had the honor of knowing someone like James Buffalo Moreno—someone who is not only self-aware but who has the ability to share insights into himself and his own journey in a way that can contribute to us all.

Debra Poneman, Founder of Yes to Success

More, Please, with Ease

by Sue Shalley

I Was Filled with Shame, Fear, and Desperation!

One day in 2009 there was a knock on our company's door. A woman identified herself as an IRS agent; she needed to speak with the owners, with me or my husband. She wanted to know if I could write a check for money we owed for back taxes and if I couldn't she was there to close us down. To make the moment worse, our employees heard her say she was from the IRS; I could see their apprehension.

My husband and I had created an architectural services business—Field Services Unlimited (FSU)—and in ten years won contracts with national retailers including H&R Block, Jack in the Box, Bank of America, ExxonMobil, and Countrywide Mortgage. Around 2008 in the middle of the Great Recession, our business slowed down. Retailers weren't expanding or remodeling. We struggled to keep working, employing staff, and paying our bills.

Despite our best efforts, we were behind on our taxes and receiving letters from the IRS. At first, I didn't do anything—it was too daunting. When we started receiving demand letters, I went to a tax attorney. He looked at our financial statement and told me, "You're insolvent."

I burst into tears. We had done so well and now, we were insolvent? I felt so desperate and afraid!

The IRS agent and I talked about our business, how long we had been operating, how many people we employed, who our clients were, and why we were behind with paying our taxes. After almost an hour she said, "Here's what I'm going to do: I won't close you down. You can keep your company name and continue doing business, but you must change your corporate structure and how you file taxes. You are obligated to enter into a payment agreement, which will include past due taxes, interest, and penalties."

I couldn't believe it! Not only had the business been given a second chance to continue and catch up, so had I. I was fifty-four years old and corporations who were hiring were not looking for older workers my age. I had asked for help, and this was more than I imagined could happen.

No matter what the problem, a miracle can solve it.
Remember to ask for one.

Marianne Williamson

Stick-to-Itiveness

I was so grateful for the opportunity to grow the business anew! It was back to basics to recreate the steps we executed when we founded FSU.

My first task was to ask our old clients for referrals, create connections with new prospects, cold-call, cold e-mail, and repeat.

I always thought I was a good listener, but I realized I could do better when I missed a potential customer's cues because I was so busy planning what I'd say next. l lost the opportunity. That was a humbling reminder to really listen.

I can't say that I love cold-calling and asking for business. Even after being in sales for most of my life, my stomach still clenches. I think most of us feel angst, asking people to buy something from us, but I knew I had to take action to rebuild.

My husband gave me a beautiful shawl with a hand-painted tiger on it. Every morning as I was leaving for the office, he asked me, "Are you going to be a tiger today?"

Well, why not! I could cower and quit. Or be audacious and ask for new projects.

I was determined to create tantalizing strategies to get yes responses from our outreach. One was to send cookies in paint cans (our clients are construction managers and designers). Another was to identify prospects on LinkedIn and send them InMails with unusual, tantalizing headlines. With every contact, we worked to serve and provide value instead of just introducing our products and trying to make the sale.

Our best strategy was our persistence, our stick-to-itiveness. By not giving up, despite objections and countless noes, we refused to take no personally, and continued contacting many, many prospects and following up relentlessly.

Yes! In the following years, our approaches worked, and we were awarded contracts with Wendy's, Walgreens, Rite Aid, 7-Eleven, Starbucks, and others. As per a non-disclosure agreement, we are not allowed to say the name of one client; think of the name of a big river in South America. I'm especially proud that we won their business. They remain a client as they open more brick-and-mortar stores. We are now a multi-million-dollar company and we kept our agreement with the IRS.

Is This All There Is?

Although rejuvenating the business was a huge relief, it was exhausting and stressful. Multiple doses of red wine every evening were my stress relievers of choice. Unfortunately, I was often impatient, upset, and angry (which became known as "Opening a Can of Sue"). I wasn't fun to be around or I wasn't having fun. I felt besieged by the responsibilities of turning the business around, dealing with cash flow, paying off debt. It was all-consuming. I felt like I was drowning.

FSU was my baby and our retirement program since my husband and I had pledged all our assets to keep it operating; so I forced myself forward despite being burned out. I doubted whether selling FSU's services was the best thing for me. It certainly wasn't soulful, making me happy, or serving the world.

A Blessing, Not a Misfortune!

In 2017 I was given a new, unexpected challenge that ended up being a gift. On the morning of Cinco de Mayo, I felt off; I was grumpier than usual.

Once I reached the office, I became unintelligible and so dizzy. My head hurt! I remember being cheerful when my bookkeeper said she was taking me to the emergency room.

Happy to go to the hospital? That's not normal.

Right away I was hooked up to machines, given an MRI, told that my brain was bleeding. I was experiencing seizures. At the time, I couldn't remember whether the doctors said seizure or stroke, so I told everyone I'd had a Seizure Salad. Humor was my way of making a scary situation lighter.

In the hospital, I remember thinking I could either focus on the pain and fear or I could act as my mother did when she had terminal cancer. She was kind, gracious, and upbeat. She stayed steadfast in her belief that great things were going to happen no matter the prognosis. I wanted to be like my mom.

At first, the neurologist thought I needed brain surgery, but later he decided the lesion that caused the brain bleed was in such a risky location that surgery could cause serious damage. Instead, he prescribed less stress, less wine, better adherence to healthy habits, medication, and regular tests. In addition to taking better care of myself physically, I spent more time doing the things I love—gardening, day trips to the mountains, entertaining, and cooking.

I worked with a business coach to help restructure FSU so we operated more efficiently and profitably. He also coached me to let go of thinking I had to do everything myself, to delegate better, and be more judicious about what I thought I could accomplish in a day.

This reduced my stress greatly.

I was very thankful to be recovering and healing—that was better than brain surgery!

As the seizures diminished, I looked the same to someone else but I was often wobbly, I couldn't remember things or think strategically, I wasn't as strong as before, and I wept a lot. I was functioning but I felt lost and unsure. I didn't want to be ungrateful, but I didn't know how things could get better than this.

It Is Possible to Design the Life I Want to Live

I kept receiving emails about Your Year of Miracles, a program that professes to help create purpose, prosperity, and miracles. Before having seizure salads, I would have guffawed at the claims but now these were the things I wanted. I knew I couldn't continue as before, nor did I want to.

After more e-mails, I joined the program.

Your Year of Miracles opened a new and amazing world of love, fun, purpose, and adventure through the information taught and the sisterhood with whom I am still able to connect. The Universe continues to answer with generosity and joy about how life does get better, especially when I'm curious and ask to be shown!

My Sales Blueprint Is CLASSY

When we ask and are open, the Divine gives us intuition and brilliance. Given to me is the realization that a blueprint has developed for the steps to sell our FSU services as well as to live with grace and gratitude. I want to share this blueprint with you and the miracles that have arisen in my life, so you may discover the miracles unfolding in your life.

Its acronym is CLASSY.

Courage

"C" stands for the COURAGE to accept the past and not let it define us.

When friends would introduce me as a successful business woman, I felt like an imposter. My stomach would contract in self-doubt, and I'd think, *If they only knew.*

As I found the courage to talk about my past financial challenges, my friends and colleagues didn't shun or shame me. They were supportive and even complimented me on my determination. That gave me the courage to accept support from the people in my life and from myself.

Connection

"C" also stands for CONNECTION.

Having the courage to share my deepest shame and fears has given me confidence to show up authentically, without pretenses, to connect deeply. It allows us to create the most wonderful relationships.

Communicating Positively

Another "C" is for COMMUNICATING POSITIVELY. I often hear myself say things in the negative—"I hate working with her "compared with "working with her is interesting."

Or, "I don't like that" compared with "I prefer this."

Or "It's too hard," instead of "that will be an adventure. I will learn a lot."

I have learned the power that words have on my state of mind, my relationships, and my clients.

Human connections are deeply nurtured
in the field of shared story.

Jean Houston

Letting Go

"L" stands for LETTING GO OF LACK.

When we started rebuilding FSU, I recited this affirmation aloud: "I am not afraid. I am not a failure. I won't worry about money."

Now I understand I was carrying forward negativity and fear through all my negative statements. I was trying to convince myself I wasn't a failure. Imbued in each sentence was lack.

Perhaps your family was like mine and expected life to be difficult, as though success required much effort, hard work, and paying dues. Living and prospering with ease wasn't a familiar concept for me.

Phooey on those expectations of lack! We can live and prosper easily when we are open to receive all the Universe is trying to give us. That energy feels so much better and different than "life is hard." I had to change my mindset for my life to change.

Now my affirmation and expectation are these: "I am a successful, prosperous, happy business woman, and I am grateful."

In addition to affirming "I am" statements, if we remember times when we felt successful and happy and we lean into those feelings, amazing things happen. It's not just to act as if success is ours, but to feel as if.

Here is something I read in Christy Whitman's book, *The Desire Factor*. I find it very helpful.

Because you create from your own personal awareness
and knowledge of what is possible and probable,
when you decide what you desire and allow the flow
of pure positive energy to move through you toward
that desire, that will then become your experience

in the physical. Forms are always created by the energy
first, and your expectations and beliefs are the shaping
of that energy into form. What you expect . . . you get.

The Quantum Council

Listen

"L" also stands for LISTEN.

> *Listening is one of the loudest forms of kindness,*
> *both to those we serve and to ourselves.*

Anonymous

To sell successfully, one of the first things I learned was "Shut up and listen."

Serving customers and active listening are at the core of selling. Many selling strategies change, especially in the age of social media, but every person wants to tell their story and be heard.

It's not just about serving and listening to others. It's about listening to yourself, acknowledging your greatness, and living in your unique power, which is a gift to the planet.

Love

"L" is for LOVE.

> *You are SO LOVED*
> *More than you know ...*
> *Life loves you and wants you to succeed!*
> *You are a magnificent human being with unique talents*
> *and gifts that are truly valued.*

> *But that's not why you are loved.*
> *Love is your birthright... you are loved,*
> *just because you exist.*

Janet Bray Attwood

Ask and Be Aware

"A" stands for ASK and BE AWARE.

Due to the seizures, I wasn't allowed to drive for a year, so my husband took the Buber role (Bob's Uber) and drove me everywhere. At first, I didn't like being dependent on him. It was uncomfortable but I learned many jokes and riddles. "What did the fish say when it hit a wall? Dam!" Our relationship improved because I asked for and needed his help.

We all know some version of the adage, "If you don't ask, you won't get."

But asking isn't always as simple as that, especially asking for help, sales, money, and what we're worth.

We can get stuck in thoughts like these:

- What if people think I'm greedy?
- It will feel awful if I'm hung up on or told no.
- What if what I offer isn't good enough?
- I'm the one who always takes care of everything. How embarrassing to ask for help.
- I don't want to make anyone feel obligated.
- I'll be thought of as a failure and weak.

Then there are the days we just want to feel sorry for ourselves and be victims, blaming others or circumstances. We each have our own version of seeing things as difficult and holding onto habits that negatively impact our finances, wellbeing, and happiness. The good news is we have a built-in way to notice when that's happening. For me it's when my shoulders are so tight they're up around my ears. Another is when my stomach cinches up. Those are cues that I am not feeling good enough or I am stuck in lack.

Our bodies try to get our attention and make us AWARE that we're moving down the rabbit hole of unhappiness. When we notice the messages our body is trying to communicate to us, we can pause and change our current state and vibration.

Lately, I've been turning to the angels to help me be aware and to ask for help. When we ask, it's amazing how much love, support, and what we desire comes to us.

Shift

"S" stands for SHIFT.

I recently read *Objections: The Ultimate Guide for Mastering the Art and Science of Getting Past No* by Jeb Blount, who says that the most successful salespeople are those who are aware of their emotions and can make the SHIFT to "calm your inner storm."

Muse and coach Marianne St. Clair reminds me to be aware of my body and senses and, when my brain is "overheating," to move and breathe consciously. That's when my brain calms down and my feeling of lack diminishes.

Some easy techniques to shift my vibration include Straw Breath, Alternate Nostril Breathing, Cross Step, and doing a little dance. In sales, asking simple questions such as "How is that? Please explain," gives me a minute to breathe and not react fearfully to an objection.

An even more powerful strategy and way to raise my vibration is to remember what my mother used to tell me: "Say thank you." Gratitude is the bridge between lack and joyfulness.

> *By giving thanks, you are able to appreciate the sheer*
> *miracle \ of simply existing, which allows you to see the*
> *miracles that surround you . . . It's important to always*
> *be in the process of saying it to someone else or just yourself*
> *or God. And it's not necessary to mean*
> *it each time you say it.*
> *It will gain meaning as you continue to say it, and*
> *you will foster goodwill around you as the ripples of your*
> *thank you's bring happiness to you and all you meet.*

Ken Honda

Soulful Service

"S" stands for SOULFUL SERVICE.

At times I question whether selling my services to help businesses grow and prosper is worthwhile. Is my service mercenary or inconsequential compared to the service of authors, philanthropists, and speakers who touch and transform millions of lives?

In the process of questioning myself, I have learned that making money, selling products, providing services, creating jobs, paying for goods, and giving to others are exchanges of blessed energy. Our energy is a love story to the world. We each bring something that is wonderful and needed.

*Each of you was put here for a purpose and nobody
can do what you were put here to do. There are people
waiting, whose lives you are supposed to impact.*

Debra Poneman

Soulful Service is not just doing for others. It starts with fun, play, silliness, and wonder—for ourselves. When we raise our own vibration and align ourselves with the essence of beautiful things, we uplift ourselves and those around us.

The best way to be of service is to serve ourselves the most generous helpings of self-acceptance and willingness to receive. (Chocolate chip cookies work as well. Can I send you some?)

*When you realize your own magnificence, you will only
attract magnificence into your life.*

Anita Moorjani

Why

Excuse the spelling, but "Y" is for WHY.

We can create prosperity, love, and purpose—whatever we want—when we know and believe unconditionally in our why.

In defining why, Iman Kahn of Red Elephant says, "It's what you stand for, and for what you take a stand."

Our why serves as our point of reference for all actions and decisions that allow us to live our calling, be compassionate change-makers, and take inspired action to spread grace, love, and delight.

I love this list of other people's whys. So as to

- inspire change
- help people live healthily
- improve the quality of life
- care for the planet
- counsel and heal
- enable diversity
- raise money
- educate
- create opportunities
- invent something
- feed the children
- adopt an animal or child
- teach wellness, mindfulness
- create beauty, art, pleasure
- make people laugh, sing, and dance

And my personal whys:

- to increase my salary
- to travel
- to pay bills
- to have the freedom to do everything I want
- to hire a personal chef
- to share my stories, recipes, and experiences
- to be acknowledged for my ideas and contribution
- to take care of family and friends

Our whys aren't just the things we are passionate about. They are also about living as the Universe intends—enjoying, sharing, laughing, feeling, and loving.

When we live in harmony with the higher vibrations within us, we align with our purpose, our why, and how the Universe wants to move through us. Our why is to shine brightly in our own unique way and to raise our own vibration, which will raise the vibration all around us.

You are not a passive observer in the cosmos. The entire Universe is expressing itself through you at this very moment.

Jean Houston

Yes

Of course, "Y" also means YES. So often we say no and push things away. Instead, when we say yes, we're able to bring our unique gifts forward to share, inspire, and enjoy living in purposeful ways that impact the world.

The Aha

Recently, FSU was owed $320 thousand, but did not have enough cash to make payroll. I was so distressed.

I had been listening to a book, *Love Money, Money Loves You* by Sarah McCrum. She writes about feeling destitute when her business failed and then Money channeled her. On my freak-out day, I was listening to McCrum's passage about where Money says, "When you ask for more money, we give you more money, but we also give you more bills."

That was an aha! I realized the energy I was putting out was lack once more and I noticed how many times I lamented, "I need more money."

Given a flash of understanding and intuition, I rephrased my requests to, "Thank you for the money in (for completed work). Thank you for the money out (for paying our bills). More Please!"

With gratitude, we received payments to make payroll that week and every week thereafter. Sales have continued to increase, increase, and increase.

More, Please

Since the aha, my goal is to live in gratitude and joyful expectancy, in the energy of "More, Please."

I think it has taken me a long time to learn how to be happy, love myself, and believe I'll be given what I ask for.

I know my purpose is to teach how to sell with confidence, ease, and grace. I still have moments of doubt when I question who would want to listen to me.

It's a lifelong journey. With practice, we can live fulfilled lives of self-love and the energy of "More, Please."

Use your feelings of enjoyment as your compass, guiding you infallibly towards a bright future.

Sarah McCrum

I believe Money channeled me as well. It has this message for each of us:

The Universe and I want you to have everything you desire. Take a chance. What do you have to lose if you ask for More, Please? When you are vibrating with fear, we'll give you the aha to notice when you say, "I need money," to shift and say, "thank you," even for the worry.

We assure you that by saying thank you for what is and asking for More, Please, of what you want, prosperity will come to you. So just keep taking the leap and ASK for More, Please.

Don't only ask for money. Ask for more healthy days, travel, romance, friendships, fun, and creativity.

Ask for More, Please with Ease.

The Universe does not want you to stress, doubt your value, or work millions of hours. You are meant to prosper easily.

Bugs Bunny says, "That's all, Folks." But it's not. It is this: Ask for More, Please!

I'm on my mission to spread the message of More, Please, with Ease. My wish for each of us is that we will learn to live generously and instill the energy of gratitude, faith, optimism, and worthiness—and MORE, PLEASE—in every action we take!

Sue Shalley *is passionate about helping entrepreneurs build successful businesses and sell their products and services with confidence. She has a proven track record in business development and marketing. She has created ventures from the ground up, most recently a multi-million-dollar business whose clients are Fortune 100 companies.*

*Sue is an insightful coach and has developed a sales process based on the acronym CLASSY. It illuminates successful sales strategies. Her coaching incorporates how living in the energy of "More Please with Ease," gratitude, and joyful expectancy brings prosperity and more of the things you love and desire. To learn more and set up an initial call with Sue, email her at **suecarol@ prosperkindly.com.***

Daddy's Little Girl
by Betsey Sarris

I asked Spirit, "How can I bring more light to the earth?"
Spirit whispered, "Show kindness, goodwill, love, and compassion. Reach out to touch others, give of yourself, go through the narrow roads, be seen, see the unseen, speak of the messages and love I share with you, use your voice so others may know they are not alone. Be present. Be a light for the unseen, the unheard, and the unknown. Go into darkness to shine light and dissipate despair. You are Love. Be love, show love, express love. Love. Just love. Take flight. You're daddy's little girl."

I always wanted to be daddy's little girl, for him to pick me up in my pretty, flowery yellow dress, toss me in the air, and swing me around while we both giggled out loud. In those moments, we were the only two in the world—he loved me and I loved him. My hero. My daddy.

But I never got to be daddy's little girl. I was a year old when he died. There was no hero. No flowery dresses or giggly little girl. No one protected me while I was busy protecting others. Still, I missed him. I wished he were alive and with me. Taking care of me. Protecting me. But he was dead.

Make no mistake, though, I was tough. Although Mommy wanted me to wear pretty, flowery yellow dresses, I rejected them. I was strong and didn't need anyone. (Except for Mommy.) Dresses showed weakness. Positive sayings, songs, and mantras became my guides.

We each experience loss at various times in our lives, and encounters with death are inevitable. But children do not have the capacity to understand or even make sense of most losses.

When children experience the loss of a parent—be it by death, divorce, or adoption—a void is created, like a deep, unfilled cavity. My sense of loss, my "cavity," was never filled. I didn't understand my dad's death, since I didn't know what it meant to have a father in my home. Clearly, I understood experiencing a mother, brother, grandfather, and grandmother. But not a "daddy."

My cavity deepened with my mother's depression at losing her husband and parenting partner. The loss of love in her own life, combined with the worry of bringing up children without a father, was emotionally taxing for her.

Me? I didn't know the difference. Except that I noticed my mother was sad and lonely. I felt her loss and emptiness, because I heard conversations, I saw her tears, and I witnessed her depression for many years.

But like sugar sprinkled in a cavity over time, the hole deepened. The pain became real. When people asked about my father's whereabouts and then expressed sadness upon learning he was dead, that I didn't have a father, my cavity grew. When visiting my father's siblings and meeting his old acquaintances in Greece, again my cavity grew. Whenever Mom said, "If your father were here, things would've been better," my cavity intensified. "Life could have been better" was inadvertently seeded into my mindset. I learned to live in a state of loss.

Today, as a fifty-nine-year-old woman revisiting her childhood and teen years, I see how my father's absence was accentuated by what others told me "could have been." How life could have been better. I felt cheated out of something. And I was. But it was no one's fault, especially not my own. I wasn't "bad," unworthy, or unlovable. I didn't do something wrong that resulted in my father's death. No. Death simply arrived at my father's doorstep to claim him. Death is Life's partner.

Children, as wildly imaginative beings, create their reality based on information presented to them. They assimilate their worlds like sponges. At birth, they are the product of certain genetic elements, like the ingredients in a mixing bowl used to make a cake. What ingredients are used? Type of butter? Salted? Unsalted? Grass fed? How about the flour? Pillsbury? King Arthur? Organic? Non-organic? And it doesn't end there. What temperature is the oven set for? What type of pan is used? How long is the baking time? Is the cake cooled properly? What if someone sprays Lysol in the kitchen? Or a sickly, infectious person sneezes near the cake? Would you know?

Just as in baking, children embody the ingredients in their "mixing bowls" at birth, and then face exposure to all the other elements that happen in childhood.

Biological parents are children's foremost springboard. And then life happens.

The Beginning on November 1, 1963

I am not yet one. My father, a medical doctor, dies of kidney failure. He leaves behind my mom, my brother, Evan, and me.

He dies the day before I turn one year old, leaving me no memory of him.

Spring of 1966

I am four. I ask Mommy why all the other children have a daddy and I don't. Her eyes fill with tears as she flees the room, leaving my grandmother to explain.

Nana, my grandmother, speaks to me softly in her broken Greek accent, telling me Daddy is with God, way up in the sky, even higher than the clouds. I look up to see if I can find him, but all that appears are drifting clouds.

Summer of 1966

I am four. We go on a trip to Greece on a big, big jet plane. We fly so far up into the sky that we're on top of all the clouds. I remember that this is the place where Nana said my daddy went.

"Where's my daddy, Mommy?" I ask. "We're higher than the clouds now. I don't see God either."

Mommy looks at me and says, "Daddy is still with God, honey, but they're much higher than this. You can't see them from here."

I keep looking for him anyway, hoping maybe he'll fly by.

Back at home later that summer, I meet a child named Beth who will become my lifelong friend. We have much in common. Both of our birthdays fall on the second day of the month, hers in March and mine in November. For most of the year we're the same age, celebrating each other's birthdays as they arrive. But I always think the biggest thing we have in common is that our fathers are both doctors. Except that mine is dead. I never tell her how important that is to me, nor do I tell her how much fun I have going places with her family. My Daddy's death is my secret.

Over the course of the summer, Beth and I play together often and share many things. One day she asks, "Betsey, is that man your daddy?"

"No, he's my grandfather," I reply. "My daddy is way up in the sky. He's even higher than the clouds."

"Wow," Beth exclaims. "Did you ever see him up there?"

I think, *No. I never have, but I'm sure I'll see him one day.*

"I haven't seen him yet but I came close. I went with my mom and Evan in a big, big plane and we went way up high in the sky past the clouds. I called for him but I don't think he heard me. Do you want to help me look for him?"

"Okay," Beth answers.

We walk down the block past the spring where we always sneak a quick sip of water, past the mean old house that hates playful children and the location where the Boogie Man is known to boogie. Then we head toward the spot that will someday bring me the realization of where Daddy really is.

"Betsey, I keep looking for him but I don't see him. Have you seen him yet?"

"No, not yet," I reply.

We walk down along the path forbidden by both my mom and Beth's parents, and I see a large patch of grassland with a surrounding fence. It seems so pretty with all its flowers and shrubs. But even when I drive by with Mom, I never see any people there. I wonder where they all are.

"Do you see him yet?" Beth asks.

"No, not yet."

"Wait! Is that him?"

"Where?"

"Up there!" Beth says as she points to the sky. "I think he's hiding behind that cloud. Let's wait and see."

Well, I think, *if that's my daddy up there, then why is he hiding? Doesn't he love me?*

"No, that's not him," I reply. "That's only a plane like the one I was in."

"Okay, let's go, but let's keep looking."

As we walk home, we once again pass the great big place with all the pretty flowers. This time there are people in it. I wonder what they are doing. It must be something important because nobody ever goes there. Beth and I slow down to watch. We don't say a word to each other as we carefully listen to what is going on around the pretty flowers. People are dressed in black and hugging each other while making funny noises.

"What's the matter with them?" Beth asks.

"I don't know," I reply. "It sounds like they're crying. I guess they're sad."

We leave and continue our walk home, but I still wonder where my daddy is. I don't understand why he doesn't come down from the sky to see me. *He must be very busy,* I think. *And why were all those people crying?* Many questions run through my mind, all unanswered.

December, 1969

I am eight. "Betsey, get dressed!" my mother cries out. "Nana is very sick and we're taking her to the hospital."

I run down the stairs and into my grandmother's bedroom to see what's going on.

"Nana, wake up. Wake up, Nana, wake up." I shake her lightly, thinking she'll get up or open her eyes, but she doesn't. Soon a big car arrives with colorful flashing lights on top of it, and two men dressed like the ice cream man come out. They enter the house, take Nana out of her bed, and carry her into the car with the flashing lights. My mother says they're taking Nana to the hospital and that we'll follow them.

I know something is wrong, but I don't know what. The only thing I know for sure is that my nana is sick.

The nurses tell my mother that I am too young to visit Nana in her hospital room and make me sit in the waiting room. I want to see her so much, but they say I have to wait until Sunday, because that's the only day little kids can visit.

That Sunday never comes. Three days after the ice cream men took Nana away, Mommy tells me that Nana died. I don't really know what that means, just that everyone is sad and crying. I don't cry. I don't know that I'll never see her again.

I spend the next two days at my neighbor's house. She makes me lunch and dinner and plays games with me. On the third day, I go to church with Mommy, Evan, and Papou, my grandfather. I get to see Nana again. She's lying in a box, sleeping. I wonder why she's doing that. I go up to her and try to kiss her, but I can't reach. I feel bad and scared because she isn't moving.

Soon afterwards we go to a place just like the one near my house with all the pretty flowers. I look around and, as usual, there's no one there. Except us.

A big, black car brings Nana to the pretty place, but I can't see her anymore. Someone closes the box. Now there are lots of people, all dressed in black and crying, just like at the other pretty place.

When it's explained to me that I won't see my grandmother anymore, I ask if it's for the same reason that I can't see my daddy.

It is. *Then my daddy really isn't in the sky after all,* I think. *They put him in the ground just like Nana. But why would they tell me he's in the sky?* I know they wouldn't lie.

Soon I'm told that Daddy and Nana are together and that they're both in the ground. But when people die and they've been good, they go to heaven in the sky to be with God, just like Jesus. *So that's why I can't see Daddy,* I think. God and Jesus are invisible. So they must all be invisible together.

I ask God why he had to take my daddy away. It just isn't fair. The older I become, the angrier I feel. I never got a chance to meet him, to hug him or to have him hug me. I wanted a family like Beth's, because she has a brother and two sisters, and they always go to places together. We go to places too, but not with a daddy.

Spring of 1984

I am twenty-two. I visit my father's grave. I want to "see" him just to say hello. Until now, I haven't realized the depth of anger I've been carrying with me.

I am alone in the cemetery—at least no one is in sight. I talk to my dad for a while, telling him what I'm going to do with my life. I know it sounds silly, but I need to do it. As I speak to him, my deep-seated anger at his death arises.

Tears stream from my eyes as I touch the ground where he lies. I want to know why he had to die.

"Life could have been so much easier if you were around. Why did you have to go?" I begin choking as I try to catch my breath.

"I don't even know the sound of your voice," I cry.

I yell at him and God, telling God it was wrong to let my daddy die.

Summer of 1985

I am twenty-three. I leave for vacation to visit Greece, my father's homeland, where I have many paternal aunts, uncles, and cousins. Even though they're far away, I feel close to them since I've met them numerous times. My aunt Artemis, Dad's sister, always talks to me about Daddy and tells me what kind of man he was. I enjoy being with my relatives because they make me feel close to my dad. I tell Aunt Artemis that I wished I had met him, but I don't get too much into the subject because I don't want her to know how much his death really bothers me.

One night as I sleep, my father approaches me in a dream, walking toward me. The background is dark and he's wearing a white suit. He speaks to me as though he's trying to tell me something. I wake up suddenly, sit up in bed, and look around the room. There's nothing to see except moonlit shadows. I realize it was a dream. I feel scared but also good because that means Daddy was around somehow or some way. I'm also happy because I saw him walking and heard his voice. Even if I don't know what he told me.

The next morning, I get up and sit in the kitchen with Aunt Artemis. She speaks to me in her usual jovial voice, laughing and telling me about different things. I can't speak. I can't get the dream out of my mind. Aunt Artemis knows something is bothering me since I'm so quiet.

"What's the matter, Betsey?"

"Oh, nothing really. I'm just sleepy." I'm not sure if I can tell her without crying.

"Something's bothering you. You didn't sleep well?"

"Yes, I slept fine. I just had a bad dream."

She stares at me and waits until I tell her more.

"I dreamed about my father." I feel the tears coming on. "He came to me last night in my dream."

"Your father came to you?" she asks.

Aunt Artemis sits down and explains that I should feel good that Daddy appeared in my dream.

"Since his death, I haven't had a dream like that. It means something," she tells me. I'm not sure what the dream meant, or if it meant anything at all. But I do know that I saw him and heard his voice, just as I always wanted to.

November 1, 1986

I am twenty-four. My grandfather dies. Exactly twenty-three years after my father's death. I know where he is.

November 1, 1991

I am twenty-eight. I receive a call from my cousin in Greece sharing that my aunt Artemis has died. I know where she isn't.

March 15, 2011

I am forty-nine. Some of my friends have met with psychic mediums and received fantastic results. It gets me thinking, "What if?"

Although skeptical, I schedule a session with a highly recommended medium.

My father is the first and primary visitor during our session. My father tells me that he's always been with me, watching over me. He's my guardian angel.

The medium shares other information that is impossible for her to know. I feel Daddy with me. Has he always been here?

January 11, 2014

I am fifty-two. Mom dies today. I hold her in my arms and hug her as she lies unconscious in bed. My heart pounds as I listen to each of her breaths growing farther apart. I tell her it's okay to let go. That everything will be okay. That I love her so very much. I keep my cheek next to hers. Although her skin is warm and soft, I know that warmth will not last. I know she has to go. Still, I hold on and listen for each breath, for each sign of life. Until I no longer hear her breaths. Until I hear nothing. Until she feels lighter in my arms. I gasp and whisper, "Mom? Mommy? Did you go? Are you gone, Mommy?"

There is nothing. Only stillness. And diminished body weight in my arms. My tears flow.

It would be so nice if I could find her in the sky hiding behind a cloud.

·· + ♦ + ··

Author's Note

Much of this story was written for a college journalism class in 1988, in which the professor recommended it for publication. *Maybe someday,* I thought.

Thirty-plus years later, that "someday" has arrived. It's time to move past pain, loss, and feeling damaged. Time to move past the belief, "I'm not enough." Especially past the belief that "I'm not enough for Daddy to stay."

This is what I now know and understand:

Children interpret life through the unique lens of everything that they've been told and not told. They're innocent, pliable, vulnerable beings who create their own interpretation of the world around them. Countless factors affect children and how they make sense of their worlds.

As adults, we carry our childhood beliefs throughout our lives. At least until those beliefs don't work for us anymore. Until we're ready to change the way we think. But some beliefs we never change. We hold on and don't question them. We live by them as though they're sacred truths. It's as though God has spoken and we think, *This is how I am. I can't change.*

But even concrete in its most solid form can be broken. The largest mountain can be blown apart with dynamite or fracture due to environmental, gravitational, or tectonic stresses. But limiting beliefs? Not so much.

Father who art in heaven. What I needed was within me. I was never alone. I was loved. I had everything I needed.

Betsey Sarris holds a Bachelor of Science Degree in Sociology. She served twenty-two years as a Connecticut Juvenile Probation Officer prior to retiring in 2011 and continues working with teens as a Behavior Counselor with the Waterbury Public School, CT. She is a certified graduate coach of the International Coaching Academy in Victoria, Australia; a certified Passion Test and Mastery of Self Love Facilitator; a certified FlipIt Group Coach; and a member of the International Coaching Federation. Betsey may be reached at **betsey@betseysarris.com***.*

Problems = Possibilities
by Rolf Erickson

"**Y**ou've got a chipped kneecap," the doctor told me. "You'll need a cast on your left leg for the next six weeks."

"What? A cast on my left leg? Six weeks? I'm only thirteen years old. How am I supposed to walk around or do anything fun with a big cast on my leg?"

But that wasn't the whole story.

"Plus you've got Osgood-Schlatter disease," he said.

Now that was really scary. The word "Schlatter" sounded a whole lot like "slaughter." And at thirteen, I definitely had no interest in getting slaughtered.

"This means you won't be able to do any physical activities like sports, running, or jumping for an entire year."

"Come on. You've got to be kidding. I'm an athlete. I play football, basketball, baseball. If I want to be happy, I need to move!"

This was definitely a major problem.

Turns out that Osgood-Schlatter disease is a painful bump and swelling on the shinbone, just below the knee. It usually happens to kids from nine to fourteen years old who are in their growth spurt and active in sports and other activities that involve running or jumping.

Next thing I knew, I had a long straight cast from my left ankle up to my thigh. For the next six weeks, I walked around like a sailor with a peg leg.

At that time, my father was the Superintendent of Schools in Corvallis, Oregon. His director of school art programs was a woman named Mary Jo Albright. Since I couldn't do any sports for a year, my father arranged for me to take private art lessons with a small group of students in her garage studio.

"Me, doing art? Okay, why not. I'll give it a shot."

As it turned out, this problem with my knees opened up a totally new possibility for me. Under Mary Jo's guidance, I began to paint, both watercolor and oils. I had never imagined the possibility that I could be an artist.

For the first time in my life, my artistic nature was encouraged, stimulated, even appreciated. I decided to explore art further with some classes in high school. But this time around I felt intimidated by the other students; they seemed like "really good artists" since they excelled at drawing lifelike human figures. That was never my strength. I loved creating nature scenes, like mountains, trees, and lakes.

When my older sister, Sharon, was in high school, she took a calligraphy class. My father asked her to create an elegant version of one of his favorite sayings: "Problems = Possibilities."

I remember the first time I saw this hanging on her bedroom wall. The calligraphy was beautiful, but I had no idea what it meant.

Isn't a "problem" something you'd rather not have? And isn't a "possibility" something promising that might happen in the future? So how could a problem be equal to a possibility? At that point, I didn't have enough life experience to see how there might be a connection between a problem and a possibility.

After six weeks of hobbling around with a peg leg, followed by a year of physical inactivity, my knees eventually did heal. It was spring, so in ninth grade I decided to join the track team. Ever since first grade, I had always been the fastest runner in my class. So I figured I'd just pick up where I had left off.

In my first mile race, I came in sixth out of six runners. In my second race, I came in sixth out of nine runners. Needless to say, this was pretty discouraging.

So in the autumn of tenth grade, instead of running on the cross-country team, I joined the swim team. Then that winter I was a member of the sophomore basketball team. We ran endless wind sprints up and down the court just to get in shape.

In the spring, I told the track coach that I didn't want to run any distances. He looked at my long legs and told me that I could be a hurdler. But I quickly discovered that hurdling is not the world's most natural way of moving your body. It's not easy to reach one leg lengthwise over the hurdle while pulling the other knee up sideways, hoping not to smack it against the hurdle.

And then, shortly before our first track meet, I pulled a muscle in my back. No more hurdling for me. Since I could still run standing up straight, the coach put me on the junior varsity mile-relay team.

The varsity runners got to wear new shiny blue sweatpants and tops. The junior varsity team wore the old worn-out varsity sweats. But when I went in to get mine, they only had a pair of sweatpants left, no tops. So I ended up wearing a faded red sweatshirt that my father had given me.

At our first track meet, I was running the last race of the day, so I let all the other guys get off the bus first. Turns out the coach was standing just outside the door, watching everyone get off. When he saw me in my red sweatshirt, he couldn't help but laugh. Not a great start. I hung out by myself for most of the meet, then warmed up for the final race, the junior varsity mile relay. Four guys, each running a quarter mile.

That's when the problem of my pulled muscle suddenly turned into a possibility.

When I got on the track, I ran my quarter mile faster than anyone else on the junior varsity team, and faster than anyone on the varsity team. Thanks to all those basketball wind sprints, I was the fastest guy in class once again. The next week when I got off the team bus, I was wearing new shiny blue varsity sweats.

During the next two years, our cross-country team won the state championship twice. I broke the school record for the half-mile. Three teammates and I set a state record for the two-mile relay. I was a three-year letterman. By now, I had great aspirations for a successful college running career.

My high school coach was a friend of Bill Bowerman, legendary track coach at the University of Oregon. Bowerman was a co-founder of Nike and creator of state-of-the-art running shoes. Even though I was recruited by other university track coaches and offered full scholarships, I really wanted to run for Bowerman. But for some reason, he didn't recruit me.

(I found out many years later that he never recruited any runners. They had to come to him and ask to join the team.)

Luckily, my father had been a principal at Franklin High School in Portland, Oregon. Back then he hired a basketball and baseball coach who later became the baseball coach at the

University of Oregon. So my father called him up and asked him to tell Bowerman that I wanted to run for Oregon. That's how I got an invitation to drive down from Corvallis to Eugene and meet Bill Bowerman in person. Suddenly, a great new possibility showed up.

Bowerman and I had a good talk. Then he invited me to run for him and offered me a scholarship. I never could have imagined how this would all play out! I applied to the University of Oregon, got accepted, and joined the team.

Since I was a young freshman and there were squad limits for most varsity track meets, I only got to compete in the last meet of the year against Oregon State University. But it was a thrill to run in front of 10,000 spectators at Hayward Field in Eugene. Our Oregon team went on to win the national track championship that year.

At the end of the season, Bowerman told me that if I kept running all summer, then next year I could be a "Man of Oregon." That's what he called his best runners. But there were some unexpected twists and turns waiting for me just around the bend.

Have you ever wondered what your true purpose in life might be? And considered how you might discover and actually live your life purpose? Have you ever been faced with a problem that somehow ended up turning into a sweet possibility? Then you may have an idea of what happened to me that summer.

I spent the summer working as a volunteer in a camp in the Glacier Peak Wilderness in northern Washington. Inspired by the mountains and forests, I began to wonder what my true purpose in life was. And to ponder how I would fulfill my life purpose. By the end of the summer, I decided to drop out of college and begin my path of discovery. In other words, I became a "seeker."

The first thing I did was hitchhike across America, visiting my sister Carol in Minneapolis and then heading east to see my sister Sharon in Boston. I liked Boston a lot, but wasn't ready to settle down there. So I decided to hitchhike back to Minneapolis.

Just outside New York City, I got a ride heading west in a hot new sports car called a Datsun 240Z. It could go up to 125 miles an hour, but we kept it down to about 90 mph. When we got south of Minneapolis, where I had planned to get out and hitchhike north, there was a brand new problem. It was the middle of the night and extremely cold. So I didn't get out.

Instead, I headed south to New Mexico, then west to Los Angeles. I ended up hitchhiking from Boston to Los Angeles in three-and-a-half days, getting two rides that drove straight through the night.

From Los Angeles, I traveled north to Palo Alto to see my best friend from high school, who was attending Stanford. He was the guy who always told me about the next cool thing—the latest great record album, a funny book, a super movie, or anything else new and cool.

He had just learned the Transcendental Meditation® (TM) technique. He told me that TM was really great, and showed me the pillow on his dorm room floor where he would sit and meditate. So when I got back to Oregon, I learned TM too.

Transcendental Meditation is a **registered trademark**, licensed to Maharishi Foundation USA, a 501(c)(3) non-profit educational organization.

Next I moved to Boston for two years, lived on a sailboat in Miami for a year, then decided to go back to college and returned home to Oregon. But this time around, I was determined to only take classes that truly interested me. So my first year back included a wide range of courses, including astronomy, physics, literature, Spanish, Latin, and an art class in printmaking.

My art teacher was a leading faculty member named LaVerne Krause. She was well-known and respected at the University of Oregon. In fact, there's now an art gallery on campus named in her honor. The other students were mostly art majors who were very experienced and creative. Again, I felt a little shy, but I did learn the fundamentals of creating a woodcut and woodblock printing.

Throughout the term, students would present their art for review by LaVerne. That's when I noticed she had a second personality. If she really liked a print that a student had created, suddenly she became like a little girl. She would look at the student with big eyes, almost pleading, and ask, "Could I have one?"

The student would always say, "Yes, of course!" They were thrilled that LaVerne would want a print that they'd created. Then she'd say, "Let's put it on the wall." She would point somewhere, and the student would climb up on a chair and add their print to the other "chosen ones" on display.

Since I was spending money on tuition that I had earned working the night shift at the Massachusetts Mental Health Center in Boston, I wanted to get my money's worth. So I took twenty-one credits per term, the maximum number allowed by the university. I did that for five terms in a row—Summer, Fall, Winter, Spring, and then Summer again.

Which meant that together with my first year of college and a single term of study at Northeastern University in Boston, I was reasonably close to graduating. There was only one problem. Or was it a possibility?

At that point, the desire and opportunity came together for me to become a teacher of the Transcendental Meditation program. So I took off again, this time for France to attend a six-month Teacher Training Course.

When I got back to Eugene, I taught the TM technique full time and took a few part-time classes at the University of Oregon to complete my degree. One of those classes was a personal reading and conference project in psychology. My advisor for this project was Carolin Keutzer, a psychology professor whom my friends and I loved and deeply respected.

I also signed up for an independent study in printmaking. I didn't dare ask LaVerne Krause to mentor me, so I went to a younger teacher in the art department, and he agreed to take me on.

Well, what can I say? Maybe things got busy. Or maybe I wasn't quite motivated enough. Or just perhaps, there was another unexpected problem aka possibility getting ready to show up on my life path. In any case, I ended up with an "Incomplete" on my record for the reading and conference in psychology and for the independent study in printmaking.

One year and a few adventures later, I realized that all I needed to graduate from college was to make up these two Incompletes. So I dove in.

For the psychology project, I wrote a three-part essay:

- "The Halls of Hebron" is the story of my challenging experience working nights at the Massachusetts Mental Health Center for two years.

- "180 Degrees" describes how I had learned the Transcendental Meditation technique, and the way it turned my life around when I was nineteen.

- "129 Choruses of a Sigh—Minus a Few Refrains" is a listing of the most significant moments in my life, from my earliest memories up to age twenty-five.

In Carolin Keutzer's written response to my essay, she shared how much she deeply enjoyed reading all three parts. Then she ended her note with: "I refuse to return it."

That was the moment the light came on for me as a writer. Professor Carolin Keutzer wanted to keep the essay I had written! It showed me that through words, through language, I could touch another person's heart in a deep and positive way. As a result, I've enjoyed working as a professional writer and editor for many years.

Meanwhile, I was finishing up a series of woodcut block prints. I'd become fascinated by the interesting shapes in the grain of wood. So I took a blowtorch and burned away some of the soft wood on the surface of a board. Then I used a wire brush to expose the hardened grain, added a design on the rest of the board, and made a series of prints.

My favorite and most ambitious piece is called "Bang Plus Thirty." That title referred to something I had learned in my astronomy class. The theory was that the chemical composition of the entire universe was established within thirty seconds after the Big Bang.

First I burned and cleaned some interesting wood grain on a lot of different boards. Then I cut the wood into hexagonal or six-sided blocks, two-and-a-half inches wide. Next I cut a piece of plywood 25 inches by 35 inches, big enough to cover a full sheet of rice paper. Finally I glued my hexagonal blocks onto the plywood in an arrangement that represented thirty seconds after the Big Bang.

It required careful work to ink each little block and then get the large sheet of paper laid down just so, without smudges. And then to firmly press the paper onto each inked block, without sliding off the edge of a block and tearing the delicate rice paper. But I did it.

Inspired and happy, I called the U of O Art Department to make a presentation to my independent study advisor. That's when I got some numbing news. He was on a sabbatical and wouldn't be back for months. So they offered to set up an appointment for me to meet with LaVerne Krause instead.

Uh-oh. Me presenting my experimental artwork to master teacher LaVerne Krause? But I really wanted to graduate, and this was the final step. So I agreed, but with some trepidation.

I brought my whole portfolio, to show LaVerne that I had a series for each print. I started with the simplest pieces, and she nodded her head kindly.

Finally, I unveiled "Bang Plus Thirty." She nearly gasped. She moved closer. She started pointing at different blocks in the print, saying to me, "Look at that. See how that one is spiraling out?" She was telling me how fascinating my art was, as if I'd never seen it before. Describing to me how subtle and wonderful this piece of art actually was.

And then it happened. Suddenly Laverne became the little girl. She looked at me with a shy smile and said, "Could I have one?"

Amazed, I said, "Yes, of course!"

"Let's put it on the wall," she said.

Still digesting the fact that she wanted my art on her wall, I asked, "Where?" She pointed and said, "There. Right over the door."

So I climbed up on a chair and hung a copy of "Bang Plus Thirty" directly over the classroom door. And thereby graduated from college.

But it wasn't the college degree I was most thrilled about. It was the appreciation Laverne showed for my artistic vision, and my ability to manifest that vision. Somehow, I was an artist. I could spark another person's imagination and touch their heart with my art. And I've enjoyed creating personal works of art ever since.

At this point in life, I'm now able to understand the intimate relationship between a problem and a possibility. I've learned that a problem is not always a real "problem." It can actually turn out to be an unexpected and wonderful "possibility."

A problem can be an opportunity to go somewhere new or to do something we have never imagined before. Instead of ignoring or running away from a problem, we can embrace it, see it in a new light, and let it reveal the next step on our life path.

At first a problem may seem like a closed door. But it could turn out to be a door you really don't need to go through. If you stop and look around, it's quite likely you'll see a new door opening up in your life.

Alexander Graham Bell, inventor of the telephone in 1876, declared, "When one door closes another door opens; but we often look so long and so regretfully upon the closed door that we do not see the one which has opened for us."

I hope my story will help you realize that there's a wonderful possibility waiting on the other side of every problem. I invite you to be willing to see the new door open. Step through that door and discover what's on the other side. You may find a new possibility that will carry you forward to greater success and fulfillment in life.

Rolf Erickson *is a professional writer, editor, and publisher living in Fairfield, Iowa. In 1996, he founded and edited a quarterly print magazine called* Enlightenment *and published it for five years. In 2017, his poem "Carrying Milk" won the First-Time Entrant Award from the Iowa Poetry Association. He conceives and writes engaging and effective websites. Rolf is also a teacher of the Transcendental Meditation (TM) technique. He has taught the TM technique in Oregon, Washington, California, Iowa, Maryland, Washington, DC, and the former Soviet Union. And he has represented the TM organization on projects in Japan, Russia, Ukraine, and Zambia, Africa. He and his wife, Renee, have served as directors for in-residence TM retreat centers in Puerto Rico, California, New York, and Washington, DC. From 1994 to 2001 they were national directors for the TM program in the United States.*

When It's Time to Lose Control
by Chris Attwood

S haking. I couldn't stop shaking.

The room was dark (as it usually is at 3 a.m.). My wife, Janet, lay next to me, oblivious to the torture I was experiencing. Our bedroom was a little annex to the main part of our room with windows all along one side. We both felt it was such a cozy little place to sleep.

But right then, it was my torture chamber.

I tried to lie quietly so as not to wake Janet up, but after ten minutes I gave up.

"Jani, Jani, wake up! I can't stop shaking."

"What's going on?" she replied sleepily.

"I woke up and I'm shaking all over. It won't stop."

Instantly, Janet was wide awake. I'll tell you, in the midst of an emergency, there's no one else you want by your side. Janet has to be the best performer under pressure I've ever met.

"Breathe. You have to take thirty deep breaths and release them really slowly," she told me.

"Okay."

Deep inhale. Slow exhale.

One.

Again . . .

Two.

And again and again and again.

"It hurts. I can't do any more," I cried after about twenty.

"Breathe through it," she said. "This is where you breathe through the pain so it can get released."

I kept taking one deep breath, after another, after another. It felt as if my chest was going to explode.

Suddenly, it stopped.

I was on the other side of the room, twenty feet from our bed.

"How did I get here?"

"In the midst of your deep breathing, you got up and ran across the room to this sofa," Janet told me.

"Really? How long was I doing that?" I asked her.

"For about an hour and a half," she replied.

My chin dropped to the floor. How could I have possibly been deep breathing for an hour and a half? It seemed like ten minutes.

Then I noticed that I wasn't shaking any more.

"It worked!" I exclaimed.

"I told you," Janet calmly replied. "It's called 'rebirthing' and it's really effective for panic attacks and other times when there is massive stress release."

That was my first, and thankfully, my last panic attack, but it was a doozy.

That very traumatic experience sparked a major life lesson. Ever since that learning, the way I relate to life has completely changed and it has the power to completely transform your own experience if you're going through difficult times. Let me explain how.

You see, six months before this, I had become a partner in an international recruiting company. We located physical and occupational therapists with the training and experience to meet US standards and placed them in hospitals and care facilities in America.

Our therapists were thrilled to have the chance to live and work in America. Our client hospitals and care facilities were thrilled to have trained therapists at a time when there was a major shortage. It felt like we were providing a really valuable service.

I was the Chief Operating Officer for the company, and one day as I was reviewing our bank accounts, I realized that we were going to be short on the funds we needed to make our next payroll. *How can that be?* I thought. *We're doing a booming business and are scrambling to keep up with the demand.*

I did a deep dive into our revenue and expenses. Lo and behold, my partner and the founder of the company, who was a fantastic salesman, hadn't realized that the fee he was charging for placing therapists was less than our costs of recruiting them and delivering them to the facility where they'd be working. Oh dear.

The following months were hell for me.

My mornings were spent calling up clients who owed us money and doing my best to get them to pay early. My afternoons were spent calling people to whom we owed money, telling them we needed more time to make their payments.

We made payroll, but there wasn't enough to cover the payroll taxes we were supposed to deposit. My shaking experience happened shortly after discovering that while the IRS may be relatively lenient in giving you time to pay income taxes over time, it's a different story when it comes to payroll taxes. Payroll taxes were our employees' money. It was the money to cover their tax liabilities and for Social Security to provide funds for their retirement.

A financial advisor told me we had better find a way to pay those payroll taxes, because, as a partner in the firm, I was personally liable. And for payroll taxes, the IRS was known to come and seize every last stick of furniture, your house, your car, and anything else of value you might have.

Any surprise I woke up shaking like a leaf in the middle of the night?

At this time, I'd been meditating for more than twenty years. I'd been releasing stress and coming to a place of calm and peace within myself for a long time.

So why did I have such a dramatic reaction? It's easy to say anyone would react like that when it feels like everything you own and have earned is at risk. But I had a feeling something deeper was going on.

As I reflected on the experience, I realized that I had always tried my best to do everything "perfectly" so I wouldn't get in trouble. I went out of my way to try to control my environment to ensure good outcomes.

Have you ever done that?

It's so tempting to want to make sure everything goes just right so that things turn out well. Without realizing it, many of us start trying to control our situations, the people around us, the work we're doing, how our house looks; basically anything that we can control, we try to control.

Then, I was suddenly thrown into a situation I couldn't control. I could make the phone calls, which I did. But disaster seemed to loom right around the corner and there was nothing much I could do about it.

My shaking experience released my deep need to control my environment. I realized that I can only ever do my best. The rest is up to the intelligence of life.

I kept making the phone calls every morning and afternoon, but then I let go. I did my best. Now it was up to a power greater than my own to make everything turn out okay.

Miraculously, the IRS never came looking for us. Once we realized that we were undercharging, we raised our rates and were still able to get contracts. Gradually, our financial situation evened out. My panic attack was clearly not a preparation for disaster but rather a chance for me to release my need to control.

Part of my attempts to control my world was the need to do all of my practices and tools for living perfectly. If something wasn't going well, then it must be because I needed to fix something about myself. Maybe I needed to be more regular in my meditation or eat a better diet or get more exercise or go to bed earlier or . . .

This constant need to fix myself gave me a super low image. I was never good enough. I always needed to do better.

When things went out of control at my company, it must have been my fault, even though my partner was clearly just as responsible as me. He was the one setting the prices for our services. But I saw the situation as all my fault; because of my failure to control things.

While the company got back on its feet, I left to take a new position at another company. Janet and I realized we were more like brother and sister than husband and wife so we ended our marriage while remaining best friends.

Then one day . . .

My phone rang. It was Janet.

"Chris, guess what?! Mark Victor Hansen and Robert Allen have asked me to partner with them!" Now, if you don't know these two #1 *New York Times* best-selling authors, Mark Victor Hansen is the co-creator of the Chicken Soup for the Soul series and Robert Allen has written several #1 best sellers including, *Nothing Down* and *Creating Wealth*. To be asked to partner with them was a huge honor.

"Congratulations, Jani! That's amazing. What are you going to do with them?" I asked.

"They're working on a new book together and they want me to help them create a mentoring program as part of their strategy to pre-sell their book. It's really exciting, but there's just one problem," Janet told me.

"What's that?"

"They want me to give them a business plan in three days. Will you help me with it?"

"Jani, it's not possible to write a business plan in three days. It takes research and creating a strategy for what you're going to do."

"Oh, Chris, there must be a way. This is the chance of a lifetime for me. Isn't there some way you can help?"

"Well, maybe we can put together an outline of a business plan with some rough financial projections," I told her.

"That would be amazing! Thank you so much!! You're the best!"

That project fully occupied my waking hours for the next three days, but at the end of that time, I was pretty happy with what we'd created. It was a good plan and the financial projections were encouraging. I sent it off to Janet and didn't think much more about it.

About a week later, Janet called again.

"Hi, Chris. Mark and Bob really loved the business plan you created."

"That's great, Jani. I'm so happy to hear that."

"Now they want me to meet them in Chicago next week and walk them through the plan."

"How cool!"

"But I can't do that. You know my brain doesn't work like that. I need you to come with me so you can explain the financial parts."

To this day, I don't know how she convinced me to make that trip, but I do know that Janet is one of the great persuaders of all time so somehow she talked me into it.

I remember arriving with Janet at this beautiful, very high-class restaurant in Chicago. You know the kind: low lighting, gorgeous tablecloths, expensive china and glassware on the tables, silverware laid out five deep, cloth napkins, beautiful flower arrangements all around, three or four people waiting on each table.

Unfortunately, I don't remember a thing about the food, what I ate, or what it tasted like. My attention was fixed on the conversation about this new business Janet was going to be part of.

About half way through dinner, Bob Allen asked Janet, "What is Chris's role in all of this?"

Suddenly, I felt my leg being kicked under the table. I knew from experience, that was my cue to keep my mouth shut as Janet replied . . .

"Chris and I will be doing this project together."

Having given up on trying to control life and not having made any other major commitments, I ended up saying yes. That's how, four years after our divorce, Janet and I became business partners.

We went on to continue as partners, working together to help promote T. Harv Eker's programs and then partnering with Ric and Liz Thompson to co-found the online magazine, *Healthy, Wealthy, nWise*. Janet wrote the first version of *The Passion Test*, we sold it for a year as an ebook, and then Janet asked me to work with her on rewriting the book.

During this time, our finances tended to ebb and flow. We were entrepreneurs and we didn't have a regular monthly income. Nonetheless, we had rented a gorgeous home in the redwoods of Mill Valley in Marin County, north of San Francisco.

This house was an amazing find. It was about 2,500 square feet on the main floor for Janet with a huge living room for workshops. It had a completely separate apartment of about the same size downstairs below ground level for me, looking out on a beautiful eucalyptus grove across the way. Redwoods dotted the property. Behind the house, the hill was pretty steep, but it could be fenced so Janet could have her three golden retrievers there.

There were walking paths in all directions. We would frequently walk down to the shops in Mill Valley through the woods and then hike back up again, or take a long hike along the ridge above the property with views of the San Francisco Bay and the city beyond.

It was heaven.

Our reasoning was that it would be cheaper to rent this house and do workshops there than to pay for a hotel to do our live workshops every few months. While that may have been true in general, this particular month we didn't have any workshops planned and no money was coming in.

As we sat together trying to figure out what to do, Janet said, "Everyone tells us what great connectors we are. Why don't we create a course on how to create 'enlightened alliances'?"

And that's how "Alliance Secrets" was born. Having learned the lesson years before to give up trying to control our outcomes, we just got started, knowing that whether or not it was successful was ultimately not up to us but to the intelligence that is directing life itself.

Now, when most people have an idea like this, they spend months creating the program and then try to sell it. If it doesn't sell, they've just wasted all those months and have nothing to show for it.

Mark and Bob had taught us a different approach. They always said you want to be sure there's a market for your product first, then you can create the product to meet the market's needs.

So our first step was to market our new, uncreated "Alliance Secrets" program. We roughed out an outline of what we'd cover, brainstormed all the benefits participants would gain from learning how to create "enlightened alliances," and started promoting it through *Healthy Wealthy n Wise*.

Within a couple of weeks, we had twenty participants who'd each paid $2,500 to be part of our new program. We'd laid it out as a seven-lesson course plus a private coaching session with me during which they could discuss their particular situation and get ideas. We conducted the seven lessons live as teleseminars, and then created a two-hundred-page workbook from the transcripts of those lessons, adding resource recommendations, exercises, and action steps for each lesson. We packaged it all in a faux leather binder with CDs of all the recordings plus the workbook and sent it off to our twenty students.

Our participants ended up being very happy with what they received and one of them called one day to talk about her project. Janet was in India at the time pursuing her passion to "spend time with the enlightened" and so I arranged a time to talk with this student.

As we connected by phone (this was before the days of Zoom video calls), I heard a lovely Australian accent.

"Hi, Chris, I'm a TV producer from Australia and I'm going to create a film that will change the world."

Well, that was a pretty dramatic opening. I was intrigued.

"I've just arrived in America to start shooting and we're about to join a cruise with Jerry and Esther Hicks whom we'll be filming. I've already sold the Australian rights to the 9Network, the largest TV network in Australia. I'd like to have you and Janet involved."

By this time, Janet and I had heard lots of great dreams from many of our students and we tended to take them with a pinch of salt. Few students really had the passion and persistence to realize their dreams.

So I asked her, "Do you have a trailer for your film that Janet and I can look at?"

"Yes," she replied. "We're just finishing it up."

Later I found out that she called her team in Australia and had them whip together a trailer in the next several days. When she sent it to me, I was blown away. It was powerful, moving, dramatic, and unique.

Janet and I always tried to do our best to support our students. Especially for this program, participants had paid a significant amount and we wanted them to feel that it was a really good investment.

We decided to help this student set up interviews for her film. Using our network of contacts, we ended up arranging most of the interviews she did.

This student's name was Rhonda Byrne and her movie was called *The Secret*. Several hundred million people have now viewed the film and millions more have read the book she based on it. It's fair to say that *The Secret* has changed the world for many people. So much for controlling our outcomes.

Now, if you think that all this happened because Janet and I were well-known, please think again. Nobody outside of our immediate circle knew us. We had the good fortune and the wisdom to do a few things you can also do:

1. We made ourselves useful to great mentors. As a result, Mark and Bob taught us the lessons they'd learned as successful entrepreneurs and authors.

2. We took advantage of opportunities with unknown outcomes. Ric and Liz Thompson came to us with an idea for an online magazine. None of us knew if it would be successful. When we agreed to help Rhonda, we had no idea whether anything would come of her film. We just wanted to help her and provide value for the trust she'd put in us. But each of these opportunities allowed us to use our skills and talents so we were able to create something that dramatically expanded our reach.

3. We used our natural talents. We knew we had success in creating and building relationships so we focused on that.

The rest was the benefit of relaxing and trusting that life's intelligence would guide us.

In the East, this is called "living one's dharma."

Dharma means to live in the flow of life. You can't do that when you're trying to control all the people and the situations around you.

Living in the flow of life means realizing that, no matter what you do, sometimes you're going to feel contracted— down, depressed, sad, disappointed, frustrated, worn out—and sometimes you're going to feel expanded—motivated, passionate, excited, on fire, ready to conquer the world.

Contraction and expansion are not good or bad. They are just signals from life's intelligence, what Janet and I call "Nature's Guidance System," telling you what you need to be doing right now.

Once you recognize that you haven't done anything wrong to cause your contraction, that it's just a signal from Nature, you can stop trying to fix yourself. There's nothing to fix. There's only an invitation to be in the flow of life and follow Nature's guidance.

How do you get this guidance?

Do a simple exercise with me.

Sitting in your chair, use your body to express what it feels like to be contracted. If you're like most people that means your arms come in and your body curls up into a fetal position.

Now use your body to express what it feels like when you're expanded. For most, that means your arms are outstretched, your head is back, and your body is open.

Notice the flow of energy in each case. When you're contracted, your energy flows inward. When you're expanded, your energy flows outward. This is Nature's Guidance System.

When you feel contracted, that's the time to be easy with yourself, nurture yourself, and go inward. Reflect. Contraction is always a time to gain more clarity. It's also a time when life is not expecting or asking you to perform well.

When you feel expanded, this is the time to get going, take action, put things in motion, because that's what you naturally feel like doing at that time anyway.

Living in the flow of life just means taking time to go inward each day, especially when you feel contracted, and take time to go out when you're feeling expanded. For most people, expansion and contraction come and go throughout each day. Pay attention and go with that flow, while still meeting your commitments and responsibilities.

When I was first learning this lesson, my wife, Doris ("Doe" to me), and I had recently started living together in the downstairs apartment of that house in Mill Valley I told you about. We'd get up in the morning and Doe would ask me, "How are you doing?"

That's a normal thing to ask, right?

On the days when I woke up contracted, my answer was, "I'm great! I'm feeling really contracted. I only have two calls this morning so I'm going to the movies this afternoon. Do you want to come?"

You see, I knew that my contraction was the signal that this was not a day for great achievements. I'd also learned that insights about next steps most often come when I'm relaxed and having fun. Going to the movies was just one way I could relax, be easy with myself, and give my subconscious mind the opportunity to show me my next steps.

What can you take away from this chapter?

1. **Let go of control.** Let life's intelligence guide you and support you. If you need a "how," my recommendation is to learn the Transcendental Meditation technique. It's a simple, effortless practice that makes it easier and easier to let go.

2. **Find great mentors and make yourself useful to them.** The more useful you are to them, the more you'll learn from them.

3. **When opportunity knocks, say "Yes!"** unless there's a clear reason to say "No." A clear reason is a commitment

you've already made that you would have to break in order to say "Yes."

4. **Get clear on your natural talents and use them.** How do you know if something is a talent? When people tell you how something you did was amazing and yet it was really easy for you. A talent is something that is easy for you, but difficult for others.

5. **Live in the flow of life** (this is kind of the same as #1, but it's worth repeating). Recognize that contraction and expansion are natural parts of life. Neither is "good" or "bad." There's nothing in you that needs to be fixed. Just listen to Nature's Guidance. When you feel contracted, go in, take it easy, be kind to yourself, be gentle with yourself; life's intelligence is not expecting great things from you at this time. When you feel expanded, go for it. Get things done. Jump into action. Follow your natural desire to accomplish.

These lessons have made a miracle of my life. I hope they do the same for you.

Chris Attwood *is co-author of the New York Times best sellers,* The Passion Test *and* Your Hidden Riches. *With his business partner and ex-wife, Janet Bray Attwood, he built a global brand with over 4,500 Passion Test facilitators in more than sixty-five countries. Over the past thirty years, Chris has been CEO or senior executive of fifteen companies. After resigning as president of a government securities dealer in the early 1980s, Chris took ten years for his own inner development, spending between eight and ten hours a day in deep meditation. During this time he extensively studied the Vedic literature of India and the functioning of human consciousness. Chris is now one of the leading figures in the transformational industry, having put together some of the major strategic alliances in this industry, including his key role in arranging 70 percent of the interviews for the book and movie phenomenon,* The Secret, *which has been viewed by an estimated 200 million people, and sold over twenty million books worldwide. Chris is a founding member of the Transformational Leadership Council created by Jack Canfield. Chris is a rare combination of the practical and the spiritual, blending his integrated inner and outer values in whatever he does.*

Epilogue

We hope you've enjoyed the stories you've read and perhaps found some tools that will help you through your own tough times.

If you want to get the most out of this book, take some time now to go back through each chapter and highlight the lessons each author has shared, ones that you know you can use. When you're done, make a list of those lessons and put them in the order in which you think they'll be most helpful for your own situation.

Then take the first one and put it into practice this coming week. Just try it for a week.

At the end of that week, reflect on what impact it had for you. You might even make some notes describing what you did and what results you saw in your life. If you found it was useful, then keep doing it. If not, let it go.

Then choose the second lesson on your list for the next week and put that one into practice. At the end of the week, repeat the same process that you did for the first one.

Like this, work your way down through the list of life lessons you've gained from this book. By the time you're done, you'll have discovered a set of tools that is uniquely suited to you. We predict you'll discover that your life begins to shift dramatically in a positive direction as a result.

We'd love to hear your experience. Please send us, Janet and Chris, a note at **support@thepassiontest.com** to let us know how it goes.

Made in the USA
Monee, IL
06 November 2022

17211798R00132